MATT CAMERON is an award-winning playwright and screenwriter. His plays include *Tear from a Glass Eye*, winner of the Wal Cherry Play of the Year Award with productions by Playbox, Black Swan and the Gate Theatre in London, where he was nominated Most Promising Playwright in the Evening Standard Awards; *Footprints on Water*, winner of the British Council International New Playwriting Award with productions by Neonheart, Griffin and La Mama; *Mr Melancholy*, winner of the ANPC/New Dramatists Award with productions by Griffin, La Boite, Chameleon, New York Stage & Film in New York, Theatre de l'Erre in Paris and Teatr Ad Spectatores in Poland; and *The Eskimo Calling*, produced by Neonheart and Belvoir B Sharp. *Hinterland*, nominated for the NSW Premier's Literary Award; *Man the Balloon*, nominated for the Victorian Premier's Literary Award; and a short play *Whispering Death* were all produced by Melbourne Theatre Company. *Poor Boy*, featuring the songs of Tim Finn, was nominated for the Victorian Premier's Literary Award and co-produced by Melbourne and Sydney Theatre Companies. *Ruby Moon* was nominated for the Queensland Premier's Literary Award and has been produced by Playbox, Neonheart, Queensland Theatre Company, Melbourne Theatre Company, Sydney Theatre Company, State Theatre Company of South Australia, Northern Stage in England and Théâtre Claque in Switzerland. Screen credits include *Jack Irish*, *Seachange*, *Crashburn* and the AWGIE award-winning *Introducing Gary Petty*.

From left: Andrew S. Gilbert as Enzo, Odile Le Clezio as Dolores, Lech Mackiewicz as Ollie and Jennifer Vuletic as Margot in the 1995 Griffin Theatre Company production of Mr Melancholy *in Sydney. (Photo: Robert McFarlane.)*

Mr Melancholy | Footprints on Water

Matt Cameron

CURRENCY PRESS
The performing arts publisher

CURRENCY PLAYS

First published in 2012
by Currency Press Pty Ltd,
PO Box 2287, Strawberry Hills, NSW, 2012, Australia
enquiries@currency.com.au
www.currency.com.au

Reprinted 2019

Copyright © Matt Cameron, 2012

COPYING FOR EDUCATIONAL PURPOSES

The Australian *Copyright Act 1968* (Act) allows a maximum of one chapter or 10% of this book, whichever is the greater, to be copied by any educational institution for its educational purposes provided that that educational institution (or the body that administers it) has given a remuneration notice to Copyright Agency (CA) under the Act.

For details of the CA licence for educational institutions contact CA, 11/66 Goulburn Street, Sydney, NSW, 2000; tel: within Australia 1800 066 844 toll free; outside Australia 61 2 9394 7600; fax: 61 2 9394 7601; email: info@copyright.com.au

COPYING FOR OTHER PURPOSES

Except as permitted under the Act, for example a fair dealing for the purposes of study, research, criticism or review, no part of this book may be reproduced, stored in a retrieval system, or transmitted in any form or by any means without prior written permission. All enquiries should be made to the publisher at the address above.

Any performance or public reading of *Mr Melancholy* or *Footprints on Water* is forbidden unless a licence has been received from the author or the author's agent. The purchase of this book in no way gives the purchaser the right to perform the play in public, whether by means of a staged production or a reading. All applications for public performance should be addressed to the author c/– Currency Press.

NATIONAL LIBRARY OF AUSTRALIA CIP DATA

Author: Cameron, Matt, 1969–
Title: Footprints on water ; Mr melancholy / Matt Cameron.
ISBN: 9780868199399 (pbk.).
Subjects: Australian drama.
Dewey Number: A822.3

Contents

INTRODUCTION	
Joanna Murray-Smith	vii
FOREWORD	
Matt Cameron	xi
MR MELANCHOLY	1
Act One	5
Act Two	35
FOOTPRINTS ON WATER	63
Act One	67
Act Two	100

Typeset by Dean Nottle for Currency Press.
Front cover photograph by Robert McFarlane (www.robertmcfarlanephotos.com)
Cover design by Katy Wall for Currency Press.
Cover images: (front) Lech Mackiewicz as Ollie and Andrew S. Gilbert as Enzo in the 1995 Griffin Theatre Company production of *Mr Melancholy* in Sydney (Photo: Robert McFarlane); and (back) Helen Thomson as Lena and Richard Sydenham as Errol in the 1999 Griffin Theatre Company production of *Footprints on Water* in Sydney. (Photo: Tracey Schramm).

Currency Press acknowledges the Traditional Owners of the Country on which we live and work. We pay our respects to all Aboriginal and Torres Strait Islander Elders, past and present.

From left: Sarah Woods as Agnes, David Roberts as Noel, Marta Dusseldorp as Edie, Richard Sydenham as Errol and Helen Thomson as Lena in the 1999 Griffin Theatre Company production of Footprints on Water *in Sydney. (Photo: Tracey Schramm.)*

INTRODUCTION

Was there ever a better first line to a play than 'I'm stealing a beach'? It's hardly surprising that this eccentric opener to *Mr Melancholy* comes from Matt Cameron, the Australian master of irony. Later, Dolores, a washed-up clown, asks Ollie why, exactly, he is stealing a beach. 'A man needs a hobby', Ollie blithely responds.

Ollie references the philosophical underpinning of his creator's predicament: a writing life. Playwriting, for the most part, seems to its practitioner like stealing a beach: relentless and invisible, often ridden with ennui and self-delusion, grand in its concept but labored in its practice, doomed to evaporate with the tides of fashion and the ephemerality of every production. As a writer, you move from play to play, shifting words from one pile of sand to a different pile. You call the piles by different names but they are all piles of sand, all elemental, all elusive, all struggling to mean something in a bigger landscape. Yet it's an occupation.

In this beautiful start to *Mr Melancholy*, we are introduced to many of the idiosyncrasies and contradictions of Matt Cameron. He is, by turns, heartfelt and poetic, brutal and unpretentious. He's ironic but never without wit—it's not tough irony, it's tender. He magnificently revels in the hopeless, aimless, pointless and failed.

> ENZO: Who wants to play a game? It's called 'Put Your Hand Up In The Air If You Feel A Quiet Desperation In Every Fibre Of Your Being'.

And yet, in each character is some kind of resolve and determination, a refusal to be undone by circumstance. They may be circumspect about the possibilities of happiness, but they have not given up on it. Somehow in the detail of their lives, the tiniest flame of optimism holds on for grim death. Love is never much mentioned, and yet it's at the heart of each character, all of whom are yearning for it in their own way. Even when Matt is at his most hilarious, there is something tragic hovering just beneath the joke:

OLLIE: What got you down?
DOLORES: I found out that the human cannonball wasn't human.
ENZO: What was he?
DOLORES: Just a cannonball, I guess.
OLLIE: Is this a routine?
DOLORES: I didn't mind that his act was a phoney, it's that he misled me.
OLLIE: Was he hard, black and round?
DOLORES: Everything's easy with the benefit of hindsight.
ENZO: Not much of a talker, I imagine?
DOLORES: He was quiet.
OLLIE: Pretty unsettling to realise that someone close to you is an inanimate object.

Yearning is an activity that fuels many of Matt's characters: they long for a place, for certainty, for company, for peace, for predictability, for surprise, but mostly they seem to long for answers to who they might be. Matt brilliantly reveals the appalling vulnerability of all of us who seem constantly poised on the edge of humiliation or exposure. Only Matt Cameron could feature a character who leaves himself voice-messages so he can experience the joy of seeing the flash of the answering-machine, so perfectly captured in his triumphant acknowledgement: 'This is my salad day!' Only a Matt Cameron character could eat a condom pretending it's an after dinner mint so his companion doesn't twig he thought he was about to get lucky. His characters have the momentary illusion that they count for something until self-awareness kicks in. No-one cares, no-one's watching but the gentleness of the nihilism these people breathe somehow undoes it. Hope resides in buckets of sand, in gathering storm clouds, in word-play, even for those who say they shun it. Against existential darkness, our saviours are infinitesimal and domestic.

One of things I've always loved in Matt's plays is that the yearning for something better is often accompanied by a skepticism that things yearned for are not quite up to the expectation. What we have doesn't satisfy us, but what we want is unlikely to satisfy us either. The pedestrian and facile activities that fill our existence are still to be savoured as necessary time-fillers. We might know they don't add up to much, but we enjoy the illusion and we're grateful that they fill the void. Delusion is better than nothing. As a fatigued Ollie rests his bucket after a day of sand-shifting, he reflects, 'This is the life'. There are probably better things to do, but how much better? Dolores asks Ollie if he's ever seen any of the wonders of the world. 'Always seems such a long way to go just to say "wow" for a few minutes.'

Matt draws on an endless reserve of wit, and yet unlike a lot of comic writing, his plays are always meticulously spare. Reading them, you have the feeling that each word has had to jump through hoops to earn its place on the page. Brevity may be its soul, but wit's heart is in its powers of human engagement. Through this elegant humour, we see versions of ourselves—albeit clothed in clown costumes or manning lighthouses devoid of light-globes. We are on our own little islands, peering and poking into trunks, the detritus of other people's misfortunes, the driftwood of our own histories. One way or another we make the best of it, we make our own small planets from children or friends, from occupations, from art, from love, from nature. Every so often we fantasise about something better or different but perhaps inertia isn't so much the product of cowardice or laziness as it is a recognition that our own small planets may be as good as it gets:

> MARGOT: We have a world to ourselves, a little pocket for safekeeping. Don't you remember what it's like out there? It's a disappointment factory.

The playwright constantly defies the expected. Where the threads of a scene are leading to the portentous, he nimbly shies away with a brilliant sardonic undercutting. And in the midst of hilarity, something tiny and tender and true shimmers.

Footprints on Water is another invented landscape 'a timeless, placeless world' the stage directions tell us, which even features its own invented language and its own population of the shunned: the 'Foreigners'. And yet a very familiar humanity is present in the moral dialogue of the play.

The world of the play is known and unknown, odd and recognisable, quaint and contemporary. Lust, greed, pride and envy all linger here along with cruelty, ignorance, hypocrisy and racism, but they are present in an evocative and eerie township where people play chess with condiments and the local whores are forbidden from knitting. Just as Ollie shifted sand, here the madwoman Agnes is moving water from the river into the well. Like the marooned characters of *Mr Melancholy*, whose lives are choreographed by the aftermath of storms, the characters of *Footprints on Water* belong to a tribe in which games are played, languages inverted, judgments made, jealousy expressed and rage evoked—but all are inconsequential against the power of nature.

Although *Footprints on Water* is a much darker play, like *Mr Melancholy*, it plays with metaphor, investigates human vulnerability and desperation and undercuts sentimentality or melodrama with deft and witty wordplay. The evil Gunther tosses his broken boot to Noel, the bootmaker: 'Noel, I'm losing my sole.' This play feels to me as dark as Matt Cameron has ever been. Religious hypocrisy, fear-mongering, the politics of community, hierarchies, betrayal and paranoia run rife and Matt's pen is fearless in delivering the full power of those themes. If this is an artful metaphor for our place, it is brutal and cold and unforgiving.

These two plays encapsulate the breadth of the playwright's vision, at the same time as showing us the preoccupations that run as perpetual currents through his imagination. Through the course of a writer's life, these currents form the unseen but deeply felt character that populates every play, the Zelig-like character made of the unalterable foundations of the writer himself. This character, in Matt Cameron's case, is thoughtful, playful and profound but the profundity is never where it ought to be. In *Mr Melancholy*, Dolores is contemplating the Dictionary: 'Fancy a whole book about meaning and it leaves you with "zucchini"'.

Joanna Murray-Smith
May 2012

Joanna Murray-Smith is an Australian playwright.

FOREWORD

There's an old joke about the five stages of a show business career:
    Stage 1: Who the hell is [insert name here]?
    Stage 2: Get me [insert name here].
    Stage 3: Get me a young [insert name here].
    Stage 4: Get me a [insert name here] type.
    Stage 5: Who the hell is [insert name here]?
It seems to me this vicious circle of a career mirrors the five stages in the circle of life:
    Stage 1: Birth & Infancy.
    Stage 2: Adolescence.
    Stage 3: Maturity.
    Stage 4: Dotage.
    Stage 5: Death.
So, how do these rites of passage apply to the life of a playwright?

Stage 1: Birth & Infancy

    This is the stage in the playwright's evolution when your parents pay for you to see the work of major theatre companies and you emerge gushing at the boundless talent, convinced you will never scale such lofty heights.

    This is the stage when you mimic what has gone before; when you familiarise yourself with diverse greats such as Eugene O'Neill and Eugène Ionesco and wonder whether you need to change your name to Eugene; when you are drawn towards the style of writing that speaks to you, that best serves the stories you have to tell. Will it be the naturalism of O'Neill? Or the absurdism of Ionesco?

    Birth & Infancy is the stage when you write your first play, dreaming of one day being described as 'an emerging playwright'. Years later your first play will become, courtesy of curriculum vitae revisionism, a work whose existence you vehemently deny.

    The-Play-That-Dare-Not-Speak-Its-Name will be staged in a fringe venue where you convince yourself the uncompromising nature of your work has the audience on the very edge of their seats. In years to come you will realise this was because they were contemplating leaving.

Stage 2: Adolescence
This is the stage when you pay to see the work of major theatre companies and you emerge railing against the untalented, unworthy, so-called professionals who are impeding your God-given right to the spotlight.

The ignominy of childish beginnings is replaced with an insolent belief that you are the saviour theatre has been waiting for. Passion, idealism and—best of all—blissful ignorance, fuel the audacious plays you write. You are referred to as 'an emerging playwright'.

Adolescence is the stage when your 'voice' changes; when between humiliating croaks you find a deeper, more authoritative voice. It is the equivalent of answering the telephone as a teenager and being momentarily mistaken for your father. Except it's not your father it's, say, Samuel Beckett. And afterwards all the adults laugh about it: 'I can't believe I thought for a second he was Beckett!'

This is the stage when you have your first professional production and naively feel this step is ridiculously overdue, only to realise years later it was probably premature.

Stage 3: Maturity
This is the stage when you receive free tickets to see the work of major theatre companies and you emerge generously diplomatic about the work's diabolical failings because (a) they were committed by your peers and (b) you will need the favour returned when your play opens.

This is the stage when, having stridently declared in your youth that you would never succumb to profile casting, you now dismiss such Utopianism as being borne of the fact that it was previously not an option.

It is at this mature stage in your career, in the plush comfort of an establishment theatre, that you encounter the telltale sign you have finally made it to the mainstream: the elderly subscriber snoring during what you thought was your masterpiece.

Maturity is the stage when your plays have big-budget sets resembling display rooms at Ikea or Freedom, even though the low or no budget set designs back in your fringe days gave your earlier work a raw immediacy, demanding invention and imagination.

The day is fast approaching when one of your plays will be produced on a revolving stage, the very thing you pilloried in your 'adolescence', decrying it as 'Microwave Theatre', where scene transitions resemble watching last night's dinner being reheated.

And still you are being described as 'an emerging playwright'.

Stage 4: Dotage

This is the stage when, after scanning the obituaries for colleagues, you flick through the newspaper's arts pages to bemoan the plays major theatre companies are programming instead of your own last-gasp, prehistoric throwbacks.

Dotage is the stage when you pray you wrote one play that acquired some sort of classic status so it can be produced on anniversaries or as a museum theatre curio, where you can be trotted out on opening night as a doddery legend for upstart playwrights to feel smugly patronising towards.

This is the stage when you become that elderly audience member who snores loudly during other people's plays.

And still there is no official word that you have 'emerged'.

Stage 5: Death

This is the stage when major theatre companies dispatch a semi-prominent representative (i.e. someone from the canteen) to your funeral to say pleasant things about your life's work; when the final curtain has been rung down to fading applause; when your plays, like their author, have reached the final draft.

Lying in your grave, listening to the eulogy, six feet under and sinking, you realise you are now 'a submerging playwright'.

Death is the stage when a young, maverick, avant-garde director rediscovers your plays, especially the early fire-in-the-belly ones, and radically reinterprets them for a hip, hungry new audience. Completing the circle in some humble, noble and enduring way, you are born again. And once more the question will ring out: 'Who the hell is [insert name here]?'

Matt Cameron

Odile Le Clezio as Dolores in the 1995 Griffin Theatre Company production in Sydney. (Photo: Robert McFarlane.)

Mr Melancholy
Matt Cameron

Lech Mackiewicz as Ollie and Odile Le Clezio as Dolores in the 1995 Griffin Theatre Company production in Sydney. (Photo: Robert McFarlane.)

Mr Melancholy was first produced by Griffin Theatre Company on the 18 April 1995 at The Stables in Sydney, Australia, with the following cast:

OLLIE	Lech Mackiewicz
DOLORES	Odile Le Clezio
MARGOT	Jennifer Vuletic
ENZO	Andrew S Gilbert

Director, Ros Horin
Designer, Michael Wilkinson
Lighting, Mark Shelton
Composer, Elena Kats-Chernin

The author would like to thank Griffin Theatre Company, Playbox Theatre Company, Radio National, Australian National Playwrights Centre, New York Stage & Film, The Public Theater, New Dramatists, Ros Horin, Peter Manning, Michael Wilson, Aidan Fennessy, and all those involved with productions, readings and workshops assisting the development of the play.

CHARACTERS
OLLIE, lighthouse keeper
DOLORES, circus clown
ENZO, caretaker
MARGOT, storekeeper

SETTING
A lighthouse on a remote island: timeless, placeless. The stage incorporates the beach, a storeroom and the observatory. The beach is represented by an absurd pile of sand. There is a smaller pile on the other side of the stage. The storeroom is stacked full of old luggage and circular steps lead up to the observatory. It has a lamp and a gnarled iron balcony railing. At the beach is a trunk which has four red helium balloons attached with long red ribbon. This is the only burst of colour in a washed out, bleak landscape.

PLAYWRIGHT'S NOTE
The design should allow for fluid movement between the various locations and need not adhere to naturalism but rather embrace the abstract. This may, for instance, involve the use of an antiquated household lamp stand for the lighthouse lamp. The intention is for the play to create and explore its own expressionistic world.

ACT ONE

SCENE ONE

A solitary light on OLLIE *wearing ragged clothes, a deflated life jacket and holding a bucket.*

OLLIE: [*to the audience*] I'm stealing a beach.

He scoops sand into his bucket and feigns nonchalance as he takes sand to the smaller pile. Reveal MARGOT *wearing a tattered white wedding dress with a black lace scarf. She stares at the balloons attached to the trunk. Reveal* ENZO, *wearing an ill-fitting and dilapidated porter's uniform, in the observatory turning the switch of the lamp on then off. The light doesn't work.*

ENZO: A-ha!

OLLIE dumps his bucket of sand, as if caught.

Ollie…?

OLLIE refills his bucket. MARGOT *goes to the trunk.*

MARGOT: I don't care much for balloons…

She pops a balloon.

ENZO: Do you think you could exchange a ventriloquist dummy if you couldn't get him to talk?

He opens a suitcase, revealing a ventriloquist dummy inside.

MARGOT: Never understood their popularity…
ENZO: Won't even give me the time of day…
MARGOT: Packaged air…
ENZO: You think you know someone…
MARGOT: Why the fuss?

She pops several more balloons.

ENZO: Not a peep. Sullen and dumb as the first day we met.

MARGOT resists popping the remaining balloon.

MARGOT: What's so special about the air in this balloon that it gets stored away?
ENZO: I'm sick to death of his mind games.

He slams the suitcase shut on the dummy.

MARGOT: We could only find one trunk, Oliver.

They all surround the trunk.

ENZO: [*trying to lift the trunk*] It's heavy.
MARGOT: Such a good storm last night.
ENZO: Must be something of value.
MARGOT: But only one measly trunk.
ENZO: Can we open it?
MARGOT: I already have.

OLLIE and ENZO recoil.

OLLIE & ENZO: You're not supposed to do that.
OLLIE: It's not ours to open.
MARGOT: This came too.

She distracts OLLIE with a small wrapped package with a red ribbon and flips open the trunk. Inside is a clown, DOLORES, wearing a vagrant suit, suspenders, red wig, clown makeup, a red nose and large clown shoes. She doesn't move.

ENZO: I wonder if this dummy talks.
MARGOT: I've done it again. I've found a dead thing.
ENZO: I'm not digging the grave.
MARGOT: It is dead, isn't it?
ENZO: Long dead. Look at the face, it's white.
OLLIE: It's makeup. She's a clown.
MARGOT: I'm not laughing.
OLLIE: You never do.
MARGOT: Did you know it takes more facial muscles to smile than to frown?
OLLIE: It's the other way round.
MARGOT: Not for me.
ENZO: [*indicating the clown*] She's funny.
OLLIE: She hasn't done anything.
ENZO: But imagine if she does.

He laughs, impressed.

She's very good.
MARGOT: I don't get it.
OLLIE: She didn't do anything.
ENZO: I know, but it's the way she did it.
MARGOT: Are you sure she's not dead?

> OLLIE *listens to the clown's chest.*

OLLIE: Her heart's pounding.
MARGOT: She needs to be resuscitated.
OLLIE: Oh... Enzo, you're the caretaker.
ENZO: I really just carry the luggage.
OLLIE: Margot?
MARGOT: I had a bad lesbian experience at school.

> OLLIE *leans in towards the clown. He prods at her nose. A clown horn sounds. They retreat.*

Let's close the lid.
OLLIE: You opened it.
ENZO: She needs air.
OLLIE: I hardly know her.
MARGOT: Packaged air!
OLLIE: Ah!

> *He grabs the helium balloon from* MARGOT *and empties the air into the clown's mouth.* DOLORES *splutters to life.*

Store the package.

> MARGOT *and* ENZO *scurry away with the package.*

You have a loud heart.
DOLORES: [*helium voice*] You're not laughing at me are you?
OLLIE: You're a clown.
DOLORES: [*helium voice*] You don't even know me.

> *She steps out of the trunk.*

OLLIE: Are your feet really that big?
DOLORES: Dolores.
OLLIE: Sorry?
DOLORES: What?
OLLIE: Nothing.

DOLORES: Nothing?
OLLIE: What?
DOLORES: What?

Silence.

OLLIE: I haven't done this in a long time.
DOLORES: Conversation?

OLLIE *nods.*

How hard can it be?

Silence.

OLLIE: I asked about your feet…?
DOLORES: My feet! Now we're cooking. My feet are small. These fit me though, like a glove, but for feet. So like a shoe really. I wear them even when I'm off duty, which I am. I've decided to be normal. How hard can it be? You look normal, sort of. Don't my feet look normal?
OLLIE: If you were twice as tall.
DOLORES: [*offering her hand*] Pleased to meet you. Dolores.
OLLIE: [*shaking her hand*] My name's not Dolores.

DOLORES *grabs at a white thread dangling from his pants.*

DOLORES: You've got a bit of loose thread… Just…

She pulls at the thread, which continues to emerge.

Ooh… It's longer than I thought… Nearly got it… Can't be far to go now… You don't have to be somewhere do you…? There!

The long thread is a tangled mess in her hands. Perplexed, OLLIE *looks down his trousers, then at the thread.*

OLLIE: My underpants.

DOLORES *hands the ball of thread to* OLLIE *who puts it down his trousers.*

DOLORES: Did you see the package I came with?
OLLIE: Package? No.
DOLORES: What are you doing with the bucket?
OLLIE: I'm stealing a beach.

He exits with his bucket. DOLORES *follows him closely.*

SCENE TWO

ENZO *and* MARGOT *are in the storeroom.* MARGOT *has the package.*

ENZO: I'm thinking of growing a milk moustache. Look more mature. What do you think?
MARGOT: I'll store it under 'B' for box or bundle…
ENZO: I've had one before…
MARGOT: 'C' for container…
ENZO: But I left it too long, ended up with a lump of cheese on my lip.
MARGOT: 'P' for parcel or package—I wonder what's in it.
ENZO: What would she be doing inside a suitcase, Margot?
MARGOT: She's a stowaway.

    ENZO *stares at the piles of suitcases.*

ENZO: You don't think all these are full of drowned clowns do you?
MARGOT: It's possible. [*She indicates a large trunk.*] Not that one, though. It's watertight.
ENZO: Think about it. In all the time we've been here, gathering washed-up suitcases, don't you think people out there would have become more depressed? And you know why? Because we've got all the clowns.
MARGOT: We're happy here.
ENZO: Are we?
MARGOT: Aren't we?
ENZO: You tell me.
MARGOT: Yes we are.

    ENZO *rushes to the large trunk.*

ENZO: What if there's some Bozo squashed up inside here?
MARGOT: Don't you go getting ideas. I don't want you clowning around in that. There's no way out from the inside.
ENZO: We should let Bozo out. Trapped in the dark, no light, no air—it's no way to live, Margot.
MARGOT: 'Live'? You said you thought the clowns had drowned.
ENZO: They wouldn't have drowned. They use confetti instead of water. Can't drown in confetti.
MARGOT: The ocean's not made of confetti. Enzo, you remind me of a balloon. [*She taps his head.*] Packaged air.

ENZO: What colour balloon?

MARGOT *sighs.*

Let's open a suitcase.

MARGOT: We're not supposed to.

ENZO: We should let the clowns out.

MARGOT: We don't want clowns darting about. We're not opening anything.

ENZO: You're scared of the clowns.

MARGOT: I don't see the point. How very droll to run around with big feet and a red nose, slapping pies into each other's faces.

ENZO: I'm opening a suitcase.

MARGOT: I'll tell him.

ENZO: Why salvage them if he's not going to look inside?

MARGOT: That's our Oliver. He collects baggage. Each time one of these is swept ashore, it's a gift… to store. Know what I love, Enzo?

ENZO: Me?

MARGOT: Watching dust gather. Seeing it settle and take up residence. There's security in that, stability. So unassuming, accumulating before your eyes… imperceptibly.

ENZO: That's a good word.

MARGOT: Like that one?

ENZO: Yes.

MARGOT: Look at all this dust gathering… imperceptibly. It's beautiful. A change without change, a shift without movement. To suddenly realise you were covered in dust, almost buried in it without having noticed… That would be something.

ENZO: Do you think you could kiss a man with a Danish Blue moustache?

MARGOT: No. Camembert, maybe.

SCENE THREE

OLLIE *enters the observatory.* DOLORES *mimics as she follows.*

OLLIE: And this, Dolores…

DOLORES: Is the observatory.

OLLIE: Well observed.

DOLORES: Thank you.

OLLIE: I look out to sea from here.

DOLORES: What's to see?
OLLIE: Just the sea.
DOLORES: I see. Are you alone here?
OLLIE: Yes.

Silence.

Except for Margot and Enzo.
DOLORES: There are other people here?
OLLIE: They're storing your trunk as we speak.
DOLORES: What do you know about them?
OLLIE: I know their names.
DOLORES: What do you know about them as people?
OLLIE: I'm not really a people person. I keep to myself.
DOLORES: And this lighthouse.
OLLIE: Well, I'm the lighthouse keeper. That's what I do. I keep it. It hasn't gone anywhere since I came to keep it. I'm very good at my work.

DOLORES *walks to the storeroom.*

DOLORES: Then why wasn't there a light to warn me away from the rocks?
OLLIE: A light?
DOLORES: Something to illuminate?
OLLIE: My caretaker's in charge of getting a new bulb.

ENZO *is among the suitcases, reading a pocket dictionary.*

ENZO: I keep forgetting.
DOLORES: What's a lighthouse without a light?
ENZO: A house?
DOLORES: I'd have preferred the light.
ENZO: We can't live in a light.
DOLORES: Why are you stealing a beach?
OLLIE: A man needs a hobby.
ENZO: Why are you travelling with an empty trunk?
DOLORES: It's full. I can barely do it up.

ENZO *and* OLLIE *peer into her empty trunk.*

Emotional baggage…
OLLIE & ENZO: Ah!

DOLORES: How come they never lose that?

ENZO: Are you a sad clown?

DOLORES: I put water in the buckets instead of confetti. I don't like cream pies. I get carsick in the clown car. And I feel awkward when my pants fall down. I want to be taken seriously.

She absent-mindedly puts on her red clown nose.

OLLIE: You're kidding.

DOLORES: [*removing the nose*] I ran away from the circus.

OLLIE: Don't you run away to the circus?

DOLORES: Lately I've been… low. The black dog came to stay. Well, dark brown at least. And it was only small. A lap dog, really.

ENZO: Like a Chihuahua?

DOLORES: I suppose.

ENZO: Or a miniature Poodle? Because they don't shed so it's better for allergies—

DOLORES: The point is, I didn't want to get out of bed. Hardly left my caravan. And then only to be laughed at when I did. So I went to see someone. You know what their advice was? The circus is in town, go see the clowns, they'll cheer you up.

OLLIE: What got you down?

DOLORES: I found out that the human cannonball wasn't human.

ENZO: What was he?

DOLORES: Just a cannonball, I guess.

OLLIE: Is this a routine?

DOLORES: I didn't mind that his act was a phoney, it's that he misled me.

OLLIE: Was he hard, black and round?

DOLORES: Everything's easy with the benefit of hindsight.

ENZO: Not much of a talker, I imagine?

DOLORES: He was quiet.

OLLIE: Pretty unsettling to realise that someone close to you is an inanimate object.

DOLORES: As long as you don't fall in love with them… Still, if you don't laugh, you'll cry.

> OLLIE *and* ENZO *laugh at her.* DOLORES *laughs then cries. They look awkward while she sobs.*

OLLIE: You really should get on to that bulb situation, Enzo.

ENZO: [*to* DOLORES] You'll love this…
DOLORES: [*recovering*] Is this a joke?
ENZO: Yes.

They both laugh in anticipation.

DOLORES: Well?
ENZO: Oh, right. How many electricians does it take to change a light bulb?
DOLORES: How many?
ENZO: You can't change a light bulb. It is what it is.

MARGOT *screams as she appears, carrying a small goldfish bowl with a large limp fish in it.*

MARGOT: I've done it again. I've found a dead thing.
ENZO: I'm not digging the grave.
MARGOT: [*to* DOLORES] You're lucky I didn't give you mouth to mouth.
DOLORES: What was his name?
MARGOT: Louis… the XIVth.
DOLORES: That's a big fish for a small bowl.
MARGOT: It is?
DOLORES: There's no room for it to swim around.
MARGOT: I don't want it to swim around. I want it to be still.
DOLORES: It worked.
MARGOT: Are you staying?
OLLIE: We don't have visitors.
DOLORES: Must get lonely here?
OLLIE: I'm a hermit.
MARGOT & ENZO: So are we.
OLLIE: We all are.
MARGOT & ENZO: Together.
OLLIE: Seemed silly to be hermits on our own.
MARGOT: We share an interest in solitude.
ENZO: And Margot and I fell in love.

He puts his arm around MARGOT.

Didn't we, darling?
MARGOT: Don't call me darling in front of people.

ENZO *withdraws his arm, unfazed.*

OLLIE: See, the only problem people have with being a recluse is that they have to do it alone. This way you can still go about your solitary business but there's always someone to say 'good morning' to.
MARGOT: It's pleasant.
OLLIE: It's perfect.
ENZO: And I love a chat.
MARGOT: He does love a chat.
ENZO: So it helps having people around.
DOLORES: Have you ever thought maybe you're not really hermits?

They recoil.

ENZO: We do have a phone…
MARGOT: That reminds me, Oliver, your machine's flashing.
DOLORES: You're a hermit and you have an answering machine?

A red light flashes through a slightly open lid on a suitcase. OLLIE *runs to check his answering machine.*

OLLIE: It's flashing! My answering machine is flashing! I knew this day would come. I'm popular. This is my salad day. Look at it. It looks like a Christmas tree. Like a fireworks display. Like a supernova—
DOLORES: Are you going to play it back?
OLLIE: I don't want to spoil it—

DOLORES *presses the button. Sound of a short beep.*

OLLIE: [*recorded voice*] 'Ollie, it's yourself calling so that the light on the machine will be flashing when you get home.'

A long beep followed by an awkward silence. OLLIE *departs.*

SCENE FOUR

DOLORES *observes* MARGOT *and* ENZO *sitting on a suitcase to watch* OLLIE *move sand from the beach pile to the smaller pile.*

ENZO: There's a lot of sand.
MARGOT: There is a lot of sand.

Silence.

ENZO: There's so much sand—
MARGOT: We've established that.

Silence.

ENZO: It's a big job.
MARGOT: It is a big job.

Silence.

ENZO: It's such a big—
MARGOT: Point taken!

Silence.

ENZO: And he's still got the ocean to do.
MARGOT: He can't start that till he's got all the sand.

Silence.

ENZO: Making progress.
MARGOT: Coming along nicely.
ENZO: My word.
MARGOT: Too right.
ENZO: Right you are.
MARGOT: Yes indeed.
ENZO: Indeedy-do.
MARGOT: Yes sir.
ENZO: Yes siree, Bob.

OLLIE slumps to his knees, exhausted, in the sand pile. MARGOT *and* ENZO *sigh.*

MARGOT: Getting late.
ENZO: I'm a bit tired.

They both stand and yawn.

The sun's falling…
MARGOT: The world's turning…
ENZO: The sky's fading…
MARGOT: The darkness is coming.

ENZO *gulps.* OLLIE *wearily puts down his bucket.*

OLLIE: This is the life.
ENZO: It doesn't get any better than this.
MARGOT: That was a good day.

They all depart, leaving DOLORES *to stare after them.*

SCENE FIVE

ENZO *and* MARGOT *are on lookout.* OLLIE *approaches* DOLORES, *who looks up at the observatory.*

DOLORES: Your light's still not on.
OLLIE: I must tell Enzo to get a bulb. I've told him before. It's just what with one thing and another it gets pretty hectic round here.
DOLORES: Hectic?
ENZO: [*calling*] Still nothing!
DOLORES: What are they doing?
OLLIE: Keeping lookout.
DOLORES: Isn't it your job to keep lookout?
OLLIE: I know what's out there. The ocean. It's blue and it moves around a bit.
MARGOT: [*calling*] I see one!
DOLORES: What are you going to do?
OLLIE: What can I do?
MARGOT: Oh no, I can't bear to look!
OLLIE: What's happening?
MARGOT: It's steering away from the rocks.

    DOLORES *regards her trunk.*

DOLORES: I think I'll go tomorrow.
OLLIE: Go?
DOLORES: I miss the sea.

    OLLIE *sits on her trunk.*

OLLIE: I don't care much for ships.
DOLORES: I go ashore now and again, when the circus comes to town. Land somewhere. But it's never long before I'm back out. I'm drawn to it, being at the mercy of the swell, buffeted by the waves…
OLLIE: I prefer land.
DOLORES: Can't you swim?
OLLIE: I'm not sure. Do you always travel inside your trunk?
DOLORES: I'm guaranteed my own space.
OLLIE: You can never have enough space.
DOLORES: My word.

OLLIE: Too right.
DOLORES: Yes sir.
OLLIE: Room to breathe.
DOLORES: Room to move.
OLLIE: Room to not move.

Silence.

DOLORES: Aren't you curious about what's out there?
OLLIE: I've been out there.
DOLORES: Ever been to one of the wonders of the world?
OLLIE: Always seems such a long way to go just to say 'wow' for a few minutes.

He absently produces a fob watch and checks it.

DOLORES: What time is it?
OLLIE: Oh, there's no time. It doesn't work.
DOLORES: [*inspecting the watch*] There's an inscription: 'To My Darling Frank'. Whose watch is this?
OLLIE: I'm guessing Frank's.
DOLORES: Where did you get it?
OLLIE: Margot gave it to me.
DOLORES: Where did she get it?
OLLIE: It's a gift from the sea.

MARGOT *and* ENZO *enter. He has a milk moustache.*

MARGOT: Where's she sleeping?
ENZO: Is Dolores sleeping in your bed, Ollie?
OLLIE: Hey, is that a milk moustache, Enzo?
ENZO: What do you think?
OLLIE: Very debonair.
DOLORES: [*smiling*] You're a clown.
ENZO: No. You are.
MARGOT: Can you do this up, Oliver?

OLLIE *attaches a black band around* MARGOT*'s arm.*

DOLORES: What's that for?
MARGOT: I'm in mourning.
ENZO: But it's night time, Margot.
MARGOT: It's a mark of remembrance.

ENZO: But it's night time, Margot. Don't you see? Dolores? I said 'night time', knowing full well that Margot meant mourning with a 'u', as in noun, state of grief, but thereby, through wordplay, highlighting the aural double meaning to create an unexpected moment of levity.

MARGOT: I don't care much for wordplay.

ENZO: I can't help it. It's this book I'm reading.

DOLORES: What is it?

> ENZO *pulls out his pocket dictionary.*

ENZO: It's a thriller. 'The Dictionary'. I'm in the middle of 'Q'.

DOLORES: What a chapter.

ENZO: [*finding his page*] Great writing. God knows how it'll end.

DOLORES: 'Zucchini'.

ENZO: [*snapping the book closed*] Thanks a lot.

DOLORES: I could be wrong. I read a Webster, yours is an Oxford. It might be different. It could be 'zygote'.

MARGOT: I'm reading a Webster.

> *The lights dim.* ENZO, MARGOT *and* OLLIE *prepare for sleep in their suitcase beds.* DOLORES *slumps against her trunk.*

DOLORES: Guess I put my foot in it again...

> *Everyone settles.*

ENZO: [*whispering*] Ollie...? Goodnight.

OLLIE: Goodnight.

> *Silence.*

ENZO: [*whispering*] Ollie...? Sleep tight.

OLLIE: Sleep tight.

> *Silence.*

ENZO: [*whispering*] Ollie—?

OLLIE: Don't let the bed bugs bite?

ENZO: Yeah...

> *Silence.*

[*Whispering*] Margot—?

MARGOT: Give it a rest!

ENZO: Righto.

Silence.

MARGOT: [*whispering*] Oliver…? I just flushed Louis the XIVth so can you not use the toilet? Out of respect?

> DOLORES *moves to sit on the side of* OLLIE*'s bed. She inspects her reflection in a compact mirror.*

DOLORES: Relationships, Ollie.

> OLLIE *sits up, startled.*

I don't travel very well in those. They crash. I have butterfly relationships where two people meet, there's a transformation, the cocoon bursts open, brightly coloured wings emerge and take flight… but it lasts about a day then it dies. Do you believe in casual sex?

OLLIE: Sex? Ah, sex is usually a pretty tense time for me. Lots of worrying, planning, showering…

DOLORES: The last time I was involved in sex was at my conception.

Silence.

OLLIE: Well, goodnight.

SCENE SIX

MARGOT *creeps to the beach at night to return a bucket load of sand.* ENZO *approaches holding a bottle of milk. He taps* MARGOT *on the shoulder, startling her.*

ENZO: Doesn't Ollie take the sand from the beach?

MARGOT: What are you doing?

ENZO: It's my message in a bottle, I'm sending it out.

MARGOT: Enzo, there's still milk in it. Give me that.

ENZO: Margot—

MARGOT: Drop it!

> ENZO *drops the bottle.* MARGOT *resumes returning sand to the beach pile.*

ENZO: You're doing it wrong.

MARGOT: I'm not doing it wrong.

ENZO: That's the beach and—

MARGOT: I'm returning it. He steals it and I return it.

ENZO: Oh… Isn't that pointless?

MARGOT: I don't want him to finish. He'll be without purpose. He'll leave. What then? We're happy here. We have a life that works.

ENZO: What about the ships crashing?

MARGOT: We can't help that.

ENZO: If I found a new light bulb it would.

MARGOT: Don't do that.

ENZO: But, Margot, the sea is full of crashing bodies, wave after wave.

MARGOT: The sea is cruel, Enzo. It's the way things are. Why fight a losing battle? Haven't I always told you?

ENZO: I struggle.

MARGOT: Don't struggle. It's tiring.

ENZO: Are you bored with me?

MARGOT: If it's not one thing with you it's another.

ENZO: Do you want me to go?

MARGOT: Nobody goes. I can live with your endless questions, your useless information, your meaningless theories. There's a certain certainty in your uncertainty. It helps to define what we have here.

ENZO: And what's that again?

MARGOT: We have a world to ourselves, a little pocket for safekeeping. Don't you remember what it's like out there? It's a disappointment factory.

ENZO: Is that why we never leave this island?

MARGOT: Ours is not to reason why.

ENZO: Why?

MARGOT: Because… tomorrow's another day.

ENZO: That's true.

Silence.

Margot, what if Ollie falls for Dolores?

MARGOT: He wouldn't do that. That's what I like about our Oliver. He doesn't have the ticker for matters of the heart. We can learn a lot from him.

ENZO: I get a bit lonely here sometimes…

MARGOT: You'll get the hang of it.

ENZO: But it's been years—

MARGOT: Do you know, Enzo, how fortunate we are to live in a state of almost complete inertia?

She slowly empties a final bucket of sand onto the beach pile.

SCENE SEVEN

DOLORES *is still sitting, unmoved, on the edge of* OLLIE*'s suitcase bed. He wakes.*

DOLORES: What do you dream of that makes you drool in your sleep?
OLLIE: Did you watch over me all night?

He leaves hurriedly as MARGOT *enters.*

MARGOT: Still here?

DOLORES *honks her clown horn.* MARGOT *is startled.*

Ever noticed, Dolores, how some houses have doormats out the front with 'welcome' written on them? We don't have one of those. Read into that what you will.

She leaves as ENZO *appears in the observatory.*

ENZO: [*calling*] Well, apparently today's another day.
DOLORES: [*calling*] Maybe today you could fix the light?
ENZO: I keep forgetting.

He goes to the lamp and clicks the switch on then off.

Doesn't work.
DOLORES: Needs a bulb.
ENZO: Click it on, nothing. Click it off, nothing.

He picks up his message bottle and drinks the milk as he comes down from the observatory.

DOLORES: What's that, Enzo?
ENZO: Message in a bottle… without milk.

He puts a note inside.

I have to get it out with the morning tide. That's 'morning' as in 'period of time between sunrise and noon'.
DOLORES: Who are you sending it to?

ENZO: Anyone, really, lost at sea. I send two per day, one with each tide. I'll find someone.

DOLORES: But you've got Margot. She's even still wearing the wedding dress.

ENZO: She won't take it off.

DOLORES: You know there wouldn't be people lost at sea if the ships weren't crashing.

ENZO: But ships crash, Dolores. That's what they do.

DOLORES: They were depending on the lighthouse.

ENZO: We all were.

He seals the lid on his note in the bottle.

DOLORES: Have you had any replies?

ENZO: One day. Lucky for me I found a ventriloquist dummy in one of the suitcases. I'd seen one at a sideshow when I was a boy. Friendly fellow, chatty, loquacious—

DOLORES: That's a good word.

ENZO: [*patting his pocket dictionary*] Thank you. Make a great companion, I thought. But I landed a mute.

He opens the case to reveal his dummy.

DOLORES: What's his name?

ENZO: How would I know? Hasn't said boo since I met him. What are the odds? [*To dummy*] Morning… [*To* DOLORES] Here we go again… [*To dummy*] How about this weather we're having…? [*To* DOLORES] See? Downright rude.

DOLORES: He's an inanimate object. You've got to make him talk.

ENZO: You don't know him like I do. This is typical. He really knows how to push my buttons.

He slams the suitcase shut on the dummy.

I'll find someone. One bottle, twice a day. Because where would I be without a routine, Dolores? I wouldn't have a life.

DOLORES: There doesn't have to be a routine, Enzo.

ENZO: You're a clown. Your life's full of excitement but you have a routine. You have lots of them. That's what clowns do, routines. And look how happy clowns are.

SCENE EIGHT

OLLIE, MARGOT *and* ENZO *march a solemn funeral procession towards the beach.* OLLIE *carries a small coffin.* MARGOT *is the grieving widow. A bemused* DOLORES *joins in. They stop and gather around a hole in the sand.*

ENZO: Ashes to ashes… Fish to fish…
MARGOT: Do it properly.
ENZO: I don't know how it goes.
OLLIE: We have these every other day.
MARGOT: You're the one who digs the grave and says a few words.
ENZO: Um…
DOLORES: I thought you flushed Louis the XIVth?
MARGOT: He got stuck in the 's' bend. They all do.
ENZO: Maybe we should get a different bend?
DOLORES: He was a big fish.
ENZO: Perhaps a 'q' bend?
OLLIE: That'd be worse than an 's'.
ENZO: Depends how you spell it.
MARGOT: Can we just get on with it and bury him.

    OLLIE *unceremoniously drops the coffin in the hole.*

Careful!
OLLIE: He's dead.

    ENZO *breaks down.*

MARGOT: Enzo, you knew that.
ENZO: It just sounds so final.
MARGOT: Because it is. Do we have to go through this every time?
ENZO: Not if you stopped killing them!
MARGOT: So suddenly it's my fault?!
OLLIE: [*consoling*] There there, Enzo.
ENZO: Where?
OLLIE: Nothing. Just there there.
ENZO: What? Where? There where?
OLLIE: Look, I'm trying to comfort you. Death is part of life.
DOLORES: It's preferable to keep them separate.
MARGOT: If it's not one thing with fish it's another—lack of space, lack

of food, lack of water. Can I really be blamed?
ENZO: How do you recognise it?
OLLIE: Death?
ENZO: How do you define it?
OLLIE: Well, it's when you've stopped breathing.
DOLORES: Stopped drawing life in.
OLLIE: Stopped.
MARGOT: Still.
ENZO: So anything that doesn't move is dead?
OLLIE: That's it.
ENZO: I see…

They all stand still. DOLORES, *realising, moves suddenly.*

He must be cold. We should've dressed him up in a little suit.
MARGOT: He was always cold. Cold, wet and quiet—that's how I'll remember him.
DOLORES: Should we say a prayer?
OLLIE: Does anyone know one?

ENZO *puts up his hand.*

ENZO: 'For what we are about to receive may the Lord make us truly'—
MARGOT: We're not eating him!
OLLIE: Why don't we just bow our heads?

They all bow their heads.

ENZO: How far do we bow?
MARGOT: Can we just have a moment's silence?

Silence. OLLIE *steals a glance at his fob watch.*

ENZO: Is that enough?
MARGOT: A bit more.
OLLIE: How long is a moment?
ENZO: That's plenty.
DOLORES: I hardly knew him.
OLLIE: I'm a busy man.

They all turn from the grave, leaving MARGOT *to sprinkle sand into the hole.*

MARGOT: Buried at sea… This is how he would have wanted it.

DOLORES: Or perhaps living at sea…
ENZO: Do I have to fill it in? I'll only have to dig another one.
OLLIE: It looked cosy in there.
ENZO: Where do you think Louis the XIVth will go?
OLLIE: Nowhere.
ENZO: There must be somewhere.
OLLIE: There's nowhere to go. He'll rot. The flesh dissolves into nothingness. Only bones remain. That's life.
MARGOT: That's death. It visits us all.
ENZO: But we don't have visitors.
DOLORES: It's okay, Enzo. Louis is at peace now.
MARGOT: Are you saying I tortured him?
DOLORES: Claustrophobic way to spend eternity don't you think, Ollie? Buried in sand?
OLLIE: Well, I can't stand here mourning all morning.
ENZO: Wordplay.
MARGOT: Just fill the hole.

> ENZO *fills sand in over the grave.* MARGOT *removes the black shawl from over her head and looks out to sea.*

Now to find Louis the XVth…
OLLIE: Hurry up with my shovel, Enzo. The beach is waiting.
DOLORES: Not today, Ollie.
OLLIE: Must keep busy, Dolores. I have a task, a point, a purpose, a reason for being.
ENZO: You need a reason?
DOLORES: What use is the beach to you?
OLLIE: I like the beach. It's in between. Not quite land and not quite sea.
MARGOT: It's limbo.
OLLIE: A sort of haven. Transient… It comes and it goes…
MARGOT: Moves yet remains…
ENZO: It's really pretty.
MARGOT: Read your dictionary.

> ENZO *reads his dictionary.*

DOLORES: Ollie, why would you want to steal it?
OLLIE: It's sort of a long term practical joke. It's not that funny now

but years down the track, when it's gone, people are going to cack themselves.

MARGOT: Children running down to the seaside to play in the sand… [*Laughing*] And it's not there? Hilarious!

DOLORES: Who takes pleasure from that?

MARGOT: Me for a start.

OLLIE: I could take it or leave it.

DOLORES: Leave the beach, Ollie.

OLLIE: I'm just passing time.

DOLORES: Come out to sea.

MARGOT: Oliver can't swim.

> DOLORES *stares at* MARGOT *and leaves, followed by* ENZO.

[*Calling*] Go on then, follow the clown! It'll end in tears!

> *Silence.* MARGOT *produces a small bundle of photographs. She flips through them, showing one to* OLLIE.

Did I show you the photos? Look, isn't that a happy snap?

OLLIE: I suppose.

MARGOT: And this one's a classic.

OLLIE: Old friends of yours?

MARGOT: No.

OLLIE: Distant relatives?

MARGOT: No.

OLLIE: So who are they?

MARGOT: No idea. Ah, memories… Look at them in this one, having a ball. Look at what's-his-name, pulling a face, that's so him—

OLLIE: Where did you get these?

MARGOT: They're a gift from the sea.

OLLIE: Margot, you haven't been opening suitcases have you? Margot?

> MARGOT *puts the photographs away.*

MARGOT: Still no ships, Oliver…

OLLIE: One went by before.

MARGOT: They never crash in the day. I love it when ships pass in the night. Don't tell me you don't thrill to the sound of ships splintering on these rocks…

OLLIE: It is a good sound…

MARGOT: To hear a ship scream in the dead of night… That moment when the hull cracks open and the stricken vessel's cargo spills out like blood into the sea…
OLLIE: I do enjoy ships crashing…
MARGOT: It's like watching someone trip over.
OLLIE: And the reason it's so enjoyable is because it didn't happen to you.

Silence.

MARGOT: Enzo thinks you might have a… thing for the clown.
OLLIE: 'Thing'?
MARGOT: 'Love, noun, profound devotion, passionate affection, compassion and concern for another'.
OLLIE: You've been talking about this? Behind my back? I always thought if I was a hermit no-one would gossip about me.
MARGOT: You don't have to be secretive with us. Who are we going to tell?
OLLIE: This makes me very uncomfortable. I feel… claustrophobic. What else do you know?
MARGOT: That she watched you sleep all last night.
OLLIE: I could just die of embarrassment…
MARGOT: Oliver—

OLLIE *collapses.*

Not another dead thing.

She prods at OLLIE *then looks around before kissing him on the forehead. He still doesn't move.* MARGOT *panics.*

[*Calling*] Oliver's not moving!

ENZO *and* DOLORES *arrive in a hurry.*

ENZO: Is he dead?
MARGOT: It's my fault.
ENZO: He needs to be resuscitated.
MARGOT: You're the caretaker.
ENZO: I had a bad lesbian experience at school.
DOLORES: [*listening to his chest*] He doesn't have a heartbeat.

She gives OLLIE *mouth-to-mouth resuscitation.*

MARGOT: That's a bit much isn't it?

ENZO: Now we don't know where to look.
MARGOT: Right, that's it! I'm opening her package.
ENZO: But Margot—

    MARGOT *and* ENZO *scurry away.* OLLIE *awakens.*

OLLIE: What did you do that for? I was breathing.
DOLORES: [*putting on her clown nose*] I wasn't trying anything, seriously. I just wanted to breathe some life in.
OLLIE: I haven't brushed my teeth.
DOLORES: Your breath was fine.
OLLIE: My lips are chapped.
DOLORES: They felt soft.
OLLIE: I didn't know you were going to put your mouth there.
DOLORES: I couldn't hear a heartbeat…

    Silence.

OLLIE: I have a quiet heart.

SCENE NINE

MARGOT *and* ENZO *are in the storeroom staring at the package.*

MARGOT: The suspense is killing me—I have to open it.
ENZO: You can't.
MARGOT: I'm sick of the clown.
ENZO: You're not supposed to do that.
MARGOT: Doesn't feel very heavy.
ENZO: It's Dolores' package.

    OLLIE *appears, unnoticed.*

MARGOT: Wish I'd never opened that trunk.
ENZO: She kissed him, Margot.
OLLIE: Not another word.
MARGOT: Aren't you curious, Oliver? This clown arrives out of the blue, just her and this package. Was she sent here to amuse us? Because I am not amused. I want to know what's inside and why she brought it.
ENZO: There are hundreds of suitcases here that we don't know the contents of.

MARGOT: No there's not. I've opened every one.

> ENZO *and* OLLIE *recoil.*

OLLIE: You're not supposed to do that.

ENZO: Were there clowns in them?

OLLIE: They're not ours to open.

MARGOT: We live off them. Where do you think our belongings, our supplies come from? We have to survive. Others may fall by the wayside, go under, sink like stones but we are survivors, ravaged by storms, swept by seas, we alone endure. Of course I opened them. I don't like secrets, I don't like surprises and I want to know when you're going to open this package.

> ENZO *snatches the package from* MARGOT *and* OLLIE *snatches it from him.* MARGOT *snatches it from* OLLIE *and the sequence is repeated.*

OLLIE: It's not ours to open.

ENZO: Shall I give it back to Dolores then?

OLLIE: No, I want to keep it.

> *Silence.*

I think Dolores might be leaving.

ENZO: Are you going to say something?

OLLIE: I was thinking of 'goodbye'.

ENZO: What about companionship?

MARGOT: What about solitude?

ENZO: [*indicating* MARGOT] I don't know where I'd be without our private jokes that we always laugh at.

MARGOT: But never at the same time, Enzo. And actually never at the same joke.

> DOLORES *enters, honking her horn. The others jump.* MARGOT *hides the package.*

DOLORES: I've been thinking. You all need your space, being hermits, so I might—

OLLIE: Stay!

MARGOT: Stay?!

> OLLIE *quickly leaves.* MARGOT *storms out.*

DOLORES: Well, Enzo, the inanimate object speaks after all.

ENZO rushes to his dummy and presses his ear to its mouth.

I didn't mean to get your hopes up.

ENZO: Speak, damn you! I tell him everything, Dolores. Sit him on my lap, confide my secret fears, my waking nightmares, my sleeping nightmares… and what do I get? The silent treatment.

He closes the case on his dummy and picks up his message bottle.

The tide's leaving… I better get this out.

He leaves. MARGOT *enters with a covered platter.*

MARGOT: [*calling*] Dinnertime!

She sets a suitcase table in front of DOLORES.

I prepared a special meal.

DOLORES: That was quick.

MARGOT: To welcome our permanent guest.

DOLORES: I'm used to being on the move with the circus, never taking up residence. Be nice to be still.

MARGOT: We like it.

She tucks a napkin into DOLORES' *collar.*

Strange the way you came to be here. No sign of any ship, no other wreckage, just your trunk.

DOLORES: And the package.

MARGOT: Doesn't make sense. Were you thrown overboard? We don't need a clown to amuse us. We're all very happy here.

DOLORES: [*putting on her clown nose*] I'm not here to amuse. I want to be taken seriously.

She removes the nose.

MARGOT: Very happy.

DOLORES: I've seen you returning the stolen beach, Margot. I don't know why you bother.

MARGOT: Because what if he finishes it?

OLLIE *and* ENZO *enter.*

OLLIE & ENZO: What's for dinner?

MARGOT: Fish of the Day.

She removes the lid on the platter to reveal a fish.

ENZO: Louis…?
DOLORES: You dug him up?
MARGOT: No.
DOLORES: But it's covered in sand.
MARGOT: It's crumbed. *Bon Appétit*!

She drags ENZO *away.*

DOLORES: I think she wants me to go—dead or alive.
OLLIE: She was like this when Enzo washed up.
DOLORES: Enzo was shipwrecked?
OLLIE: He fell overboard while working on a cruise liner. Margot wanted him to swim back out but she came around. She's just not good with surprises.
DOLORES: Who is? When I heard about the human cannonball and the trapeze artist it was like a ten tonne weight landed on me.
OLLIE: [*looking up*] You never know what's going to strike you down. All manner of doom is hurtling towards us as we speak.
DOLORES: Really?
OLLIE: Meteors shave by all the time, barely missing us.
DOLORES: By how much?
OLLIE: A hundred thousand kilometres.
DOLORES: Phew.
OLLIE: But when you think how big space is…

Silence.

I'd like to go into space.
DOLORES: And do what?
OLLIE: Just sit there.
DOLORES: I'd like to go to the horizon.
OLLIE: But it's unreachable, indefinable. It's like…
DOLORES: Stealing a beach?
OLLIE: The horizon doesn't actually exist. You can never get close to it. It's unknowable.
DOLORES: We're all heads, that's the problem. Take a look at any ship sailing by, full of disembodied passengers. All these heads bobbing about in the porthole… [*bobbing her head*] looking out, trying to spot their body.

Sound of distant circus music.

Can you hear that?
OLLIE: The waves?
DOLORES: The music…

    OLLIE *listens, staring at* DOLORES.

OLLIE: Would you like to dance?
DOLORES: As long as you don't tread on my feet.
OLLIE: [*looking at her clown shoes*] You don't make it easy…

    They dance an awkward but serious waltz.

What does your face look like?
DOLORES: This.
OLLIE: Under that one.
DOLORES: I don't remember.
OLLIE: You could take it off…?
DOLORES: Do you want to kiss me?

    They both look away, stunned. DOLORES *points at a spot.*

Meet me at that spot there if you want to.
OLLIE: That spot there?
DOLORES: There. That spot.

    They tentatively move towards the spot.

OLLIE: Are you going to that spot?
DOLORES: I'll meet you there if I am.

    They arrive and stop, facing each other, looking down.

OLLIE: This is the spot…
DOLORES: This is the spot…

    They awkwardly but tenderly kiss. The clown shoes get in the way and they fall in a tangled mess.

OLLIE: That went well.
DOLORES: Swept me off my feet.
OLLIE: I haven't done this in a long time.
DOLORES: It's these shoes…

    OLLIE *helps* DOLORES *up and she stands in close.*

I could take them off…?

OLLIE: [*muttering*] Dead cat, dead cat, dead cat, dead cat—
DOLORES: 'Dead cat'? What is that?
OLLIE: It's an anti-arousal phrase that I use. Dead cat, dead cat, dead cat—
DOLORES: What about 'old nun'?
OLLIE: Doesn't work.
DOLORES: Old nun, old nun, old nun—
OLLIE: In fact, can you stop saying that?
DOLORES: Old nun, old nun, old nun—
OLLIE: Please, I'm in the middle of a drought—
DOLORES: I might slip into something more comfortable.
OLLIE: Right…

> DOLORES *leaves.* OLLIE *smiles, takes out a condom from his wallet and places it on the pillow of his suitcase bed. He casually reclines. He suddenly leaps up and undoes his pants. They fall to his ankles as* DOLORES *enters, holding her clown shoes. She places them on the floor.*

DOLORES: That's much more comfortable.

> *She looks up to see* OLLIE *with his pants around his ankles.*

Oh.
OLLIE: I thought you meant…
DOLORES: What?
OLLIE: Nothing.
DOLORES: Nothing?
OLLIE: [*checking his fob watch*] Is that the time? Good night!

> *He yawns desperately.* DOLORES *spots the condom on the bed.*

DOLORES: What's that on your bed?
OLLIE: [*realising*] The bed! Oh, that's—
DOLORES: Is that a…?

> OLLIE *dashes to grab it, tripping over his pants.*

OLLIE: It's an after dinner mint!
DOLORES: Let me see.

> OLLIE *rips the packet open and puts the condom in his mouth.*

OLLIE: Mmm, that's good…

DOLORES: Do you want to have sex with me on that spot there?

> *She points to a spot.* OLLIE *nods and gulps.*

But we needed that after dinner mint.

SCENE TEN

Distant circus music draws DOLORES *to her trunk from which she lifts out a lit-up miniature circus tent. As she hums the circus tune she looks at* OLLIE *trying to regurgitate the condom then at* ENZO *slapping his ventriloquist dummy, trying to make it talk, then at* MARGOT *giving a fish mouth to mouth.* DOLORES *places a message bottle with a red clown nose as a lid on the beach. She gets inside her trunk and pulls the lid closed. The light fades on the trunk.* MARGOT *and* ENZO *assume lookout duties in the observatory.*

ENZO: Margot, is that a ship out to sea?
MARGOT: It's too small.
ENZO: Looks like Dolores' trunk…
MARGOT: [*smiling*] Oh, say it isn't so.
ENZO: There's a bottle, Ollie! She sent a message!

> OLLIE *takes out the note inside the bottle and reads it.*

Why did she go?

OLLIE: For a moment there I was almost happy.

> *He tears up the note and throws the pieces of paper in the air. Thousands of pieces of torn paper rain down on him.*

ENZO: Confetti…

> OLLIE *looks at the clown nose in his hand. The circus music fades into the sound of the waves. Blackout.*

END OF ACT ONE

ACT TWO

SCENE ONE

The stage is unchanged, apart from the absence of the trunk.

OLLIE *is alone with his hands inside* DOLORES' *clown shoes. A red light flashes inside a slightly open suitcase. Sound of a beep and outgoing message.*

OLLIE: [*recorded voice*] 'Um… you've called Ollie. I can't come to the phone right now so leave a message… please.'

There is a beep followed by an automated voice message.

VOICE: [*automated*] 'You have no messages.'

OLLIE: You don't have to sound so smug about it.

Sound of a long beep. The red light stops flashing. A solitary spotlight on the ventriloquist dummy's open case. It is dressed like OLLIE *with a tiny bucket and sand pile.* ENZO*'s hand can be seen operating the dummy from behind the case.*

ENZO: The dark lighthouse stands still
While the ships crash by night
And the sands of time kill
The keeper of the light.

He jams the bucket on the dummy's head, sand raining down.

[*Muffled*] 'Help… help…'

OLLIE—*unravelling the answering machine tape—steps in beside the dummy and coughs pointedly.* ENZO *crawls out from behind the case.*

OLLIE: And who's that supposed to be?

ENZO: It was his idea. He's come alive, Ollie. We're chatting, shooting the breeze, chewing the fat.

OLLIE: It's just you, Enzo.

ENZO: [*covering the dummy's ears*] Ssh!

OLLIE: You're on your own.

MARGOT *enters, picking up the pieces of torn paper.*

MARGOT: We all are.

OLLIE: What are you doing?

MARGOT: Picking up the pieces.

She exits with the scraps. OLLIE *throws away the unravelled answering machine tape.*

OLLIE: No messages… You know what I can't bear about answering machines? The hope.

ENZO: Tomorrow's another day…

OLLIE: I don't think I could endure another.

They look to the horizon.

ENZO: The sun's falling…

OLLIE: The sky's crawling…

A windblown MARGOT *appears in the observatory.*

MARGOT: [*calling*] The storm's coming!

A crack of thunder, flashes of lightning, fierce winds and stormy seas.

Roll up, roll up! Come one come all! There, beyond the break, Oliver! Once again the universe provides!

ENZO: Shall I put the light on?

MARGOT: Come to me my little darling!

OLLIE: We don't have a bulb, Enzo.

ENZO: I keep forgetting.

MARGOT: Bartender, I'll have my usual—a ship, on the rocks!

Sound of a ship's hull splintering.

SCENE TWO

A solitary light on OLLIE *at the beach with his bucket.*

OLLIE: [*to the audience*] I'm steal— … Oh, you know what I'm doing.

He sighs and scoops sand into his bucket. Reveal MARGOT *holding the message bottle and the note in torn pieces.* ENZO *is in the observatory turning the lamp switch on then off. The light doesn't work.*

ENZO: A-ha!

> OLLIE *continues stealing.*

Ollie...?

MARGOT: I don't care much for messages in bottles...

ENZO: Do you think acupuncture would have any effect on a man who thinks he's a pin cushion?

MARGOT: What's so special about this message that it gets stored away?

ENZO: What footwear do they recommend if you take the path less travelled? And how far is it? Should you take a cut lunch?

OLLIE: Enough, Enzo! Read your dictionary.

> ENZO *reads his dictionary.*

MARGOT: [*reading the pieces of the note*] 'Love not taken happiness forsaken the possible denied by the true heart that hides the embrace misplaced with the kiss that insists the atheist prays to end days of malaise walk talk baulk and allude tastefully imagine each other in the nude filled with daring desire and despair spending more time than ever on their hair they dim and they dumb but never succumb invite and repel I know you so well but I don't really know you at all the climb is sublime the hope is the rope that saves you or hangs you when you fall together alone maybe I'll phone pretend transcend begin begin begin and end.'

OLLIE: Stop reading that.

MARGOT: Stupid clown thinks she's a poet.

OLLIE: What's got into you, Margot? You're being playful.

MARGOT: Between you and me, I'm happy. No clown and that ship crashing last night. It doesn't get any better than this.

ENZO: Really?

MARGOT: It's back to how it was.

ENZO: But I'm dying here. I need a distraction. I need to be kept amused. I need a—

MARGOT: Don't even think it. We're happy here.

OLLIE & ENZO: Are we?

MARGOT: Don't start on me with that routine.

ENZO: How can we be happy without a—?

MARGOT: Don't say it.

ENZO: Clown.

MARGOT: Take that back!
ENZO: Dolores called me a clown.
MARGOT: It's not a compliment.
ENZO: Who wants to play a game? It's called 'Put Your Hand Up In The Air If You Feel A Quiet Desperation In Every Fibre Of Your Being'.

He quickly raises his hand. OLLIE *and* MARGOT *are unmoved.*

Did you not understand the rules?
MARGOT: Will you stop reading that wretched book!

ENZO *retreats to resume reading his dictionary.*

OLLIE: I found my bucket at the beach this morning. Don't remember leaving it there.
MARGOT: I did a few trips for you last night.
OLLIE: This beach isn't getting any smaller.
MARGOT: Persistence, Oliver. Did you see the storeroom? Such bounty. Bursting at the seams. We can start again, just the three of us.
OLLIE: And no more opening suitcases. They stay closed.
MARGOT: Good crash last night, wasn't it?
OLLIE: I didn't enjoy it.
ENZO: [*calling*] Me either.
MARGOT: Who asked you?
OLLIE: I could feel the fear, the dread. I heard that ship howl. Wood on stone, lurching, creaking… It was pitch dark, Margot, but I could see that ship sinking.
MARGOT: There wasn't one shipwreck while she was here.
OLLIE: Coincidence.
MARGOT: But as soon as she went…
OLLIE: She seemed happy to stay…
MARGOT: She's used to parking her stupid big shoes under a different bed every night. We have that rare ability to be still. We don't have to move. The world turns for us, Ollie. This is our space.
OLLIE: You can never have enough.
MARGOT: Imagine gathering all this space and surrounding yourself in it, being right in the middle of it all… unreachable.
OLLIE: Then I'd be alone.

Silence.

MARGOT: Except for me and Enzo.

OLLIE: Yes.

MARGOT: Stealing space. It's a worthy pursuit, Oliver. You keep on it.

OLLIE: What if I get lost in all that space, Margot? What if I can never find my way out?

MARGOT: What a way to go.

> ENZO *snaps the book shut and throws it to the ground.*

OLLIE: Finished?

ENZO: There's no point. Ultimately it doesn't mean anything. I know how it ends.

OLLIE: I know how lots of things will end, doesn't stop me doing them. I spend every day taking the sand from here to there.

MARGOT: We can learn a lot from this man.

ENZO: How does it end?

OLLIE: It doesn't. It just keeps going. There is no end.

MARGOT: No surprises. No unknowns. No wonder we're happy here.

> *She departs.* OLLIE *puts his head in his hands and weeps. A frightened* ENZO *watches.*

ENZO: Ollie…? Please… don't… Ollie…?

> *He dissolves.*

Are you not happy here…?

OLLIE: Perish the thought.

ENZO: But you're cry—

OLLIE: No I'm not. [*He tries to gather himself.*] Look at us, Enzo. Living the life. What more could we ask for? We're having our cake and we're eating it too!

ENZO: [*relieved, cheering up*] Oh! You had me worried.

> *They each blow their nose into a handkerchief and take a deep breath.*

Ollie…? Do you think there's a whole circus in those suitcases we've got stored? At first I thought it was just clowns but maybe it's the whole troupe? Strong men, fat ladies, knife throwers, trapeze artists, elephants—?

OLLIE: Margot's opened them all.

ENZO: Maybe she's not telling us. Maybe we're this close to a circus and we don't even know it.

OLLIE: I don't want to talk about the circus.

> *Silence.* ENZO *hums the circus tune.* OLLIE *covers* ENZO*'s mouth. He stops humming.*

I thought I was past all this.

ENZO: What?

OLLIE: Dependence. That's why I came here. It's remote. It's just me.

> *Silence.*

ENZO: And me and Margot.

OLLIE: Yes…

ENZO: If we had a light, nothing would come near us. Every ship would steer away.

OLLIE: You're the caretaker. I've told you to replace the bulb.

ENZO: You like getting these suitcases washed up.

OLLIE: It's got nothing to do with me. I can't be blamed. The seas change, storms rage, ships crash. It distresses me.

> *Silence.*

ENZO: Ollie?

OLLIE: Yes, Enzo?

ENZO: How come I didn't get any cake?

SCENE THREE

MARGOT *prepares to drop another limp fish into a sandy grave as* OLLIE *approaches.*

OLLIE: Oh Margot, not Louis the XVth?

MARGOT: I can't seem to keep anything alive.

> *She drops the fish in the hole.* OLLIE *ties another black armband onto her arm.*

My whole life is a near death experience.

> *She pushes sand over the hole. They share a reverent silence.*

OLLIE: I remember once being buried up to my neck at the beach…

MARGOT: I've heard of that. On summer holidays. People do it for fun.

OLLIE: Except I was buried head first.

MARGOT: See, Ollie? No good ever comes of fun.

She pats down the sand.

OLLIE: Do things seem different to you, Margot?
MARGOT: No, they're the same. They seem the same.

ENZO appears, dragging a suitcase.

OLLIE: What have you got there, Enzo?

ENZO stops to catch his breath and begins to laugh.

MARGOT: Are you laughing?
ENZO: If you don't laugh you'll cry.

His laughter turns to tears.

MARGOT: Pull yourself together.
ENZO: I found them washed up on the far shore.
OLLIE: Found what?

ENZO goes to flip open the suitcase.

Whoa! You can't just open it!
ENZO: Trust me, you need to see this.

He opens the case. They all stare inside, stunned.

Do you think they belong to… her?
OLLIE: She was in a trunk.
ENZO: I didn't find them in this suitcase. They were scattered on the sand.
OLLIE: We can't even be sure these all belong to the same person.

He takes out a human bone from the suitcase.

How long has she been gone?

MARGOT and ENZO take out more human bones.

ENZO: This is our doing.
MARGOT: The sea is a cruel mistress.
ENZO: How many times have we watched them founder?
MARGOT: We're hanging on for dear life ourselves.
ENZO: How many times have we ignored their cries for help?
MARGOT: You can't even hear yourself think in the middle of a storm.
OLLIE: I will not be blamed for strangers dashed against rocks, intrepid travellers who should've known better the devils in the deep blue sea, how she swallows all who dare cross her, chews them up and spits them out… Close the suitcase, Enzo.

ENZO: But Ollie—
OLLIE: Close it!

They return the bones. ENZO *closes the suitcase.*

MARGOT: What are we going to do?
OLLIE: Take it to the storeroom, find a dark corner, bury it. Then let us never speak of this again.

ENZO and MARGOT drag the suitcase to the storeroom. OLLIE *is left alone, staring out to sea. He climbs up to the observatory and stares at the lamp.*

What use is a little light against all this roaring, churning might?

ENZO and MARGOT are in the storeroom staring intently at the package.

MARGOT: [*calling*] Oliver! She didn't take her package.

OLLIE *approaches and takes it.*

ENZO: She never knew we had it.
OLLIE: I think she did.
MARGOT: Can I open it?
OLLIE: It's not ours to open.
ENZO: Do you think the sea took her, Ollie?
OLLIE: I fear the worst.
ENZO: So do I.
MARGOT: It's what we do. It's why we prefer not to move.

ENZO *moves suddenly.* OLLIE *and* MARGOT *remain still.*

I know what's missing here—dust! It's been unsettled. How can we tell where everything belongs unless we have dust to mark where it's always been?

OLLIE: Time will pass, Margot, inevitably, inexorably. And the remains of long dead days will surreptitiously settle and once again no-one will see us for dust.
MARGOT: Well, yes, but why wait?

She holds up a message bottle filled with white dust.

I stored it. I bottled it.

ENZO: Not my message bottle?
MARGOT: I don't want you sending these out.

ENZO: I don't want your dust in my bottle.
MARGOT: Neither do I.

> *She flings the dust in the air.* ENZO *and* OLLIE *cough as the white dust falls on them.*

OLLIE: What are you doing, Margot?
MARGOT: I'm dusting.
ENZO: I can't breathe.
MARGOT: Stop coughing and let it settle. Look at all this dust gathering…

> OLLIE, ENZO *and* MARGOT *are lost in a thick cloud of dust.*

ENZO: What happened to 'imperceptibly'?
MARGOT: We're buried in it…

> *The dust settles on them.*

Same as it ever was.
OLLIE: It doesn't get any better than this.
MARGOT: Just we three.
ENZO: Not quite.

> *He points to a still figure in a crumpled jacket and skirt, holding up a hole-ridden umbrella, covered with dust. It is an almost unrecognisable* DOLORES, *without her clown attire.* OLLIE *hides the package.*

MARGOT: Who are you?
DOLORES: Who are you?
ENZO: Who are we?
OLLIE: We're hermits.

> DOLORES *releases the umbrella as she steps away. It remains suspended in mid-air before drifting skywards.*

You look familiar.
MARGOT: You have a familiar face.
DOLORES: I have one of those faces.
ENZO: That's true, she does.
DOLORES: The kind of face people recognise: nose, two eyes, a mouth.
ENZO: Ah yes, that's it! I couldn't put my finger on it.
OLLIE: We never forget a face.
MARGOT: We forget our own faces.

DOLORES: I looked in the mirror today and I saw a stranger staring back.

ENZO: Same thing happened to me!

OLLIE: Enzo, you were looking out a window.

MARGOT: At me.

ENZO: Ah!

MARGOT: You're not planning on staying are you?

DOLORES: I am a qualified hermit.

ENZO: The more hermits the merrier.

OLLIE: Are you experienced?

MARGOT: Do you have references?

ENZO: We maintain the highest of standards here.

OLLIE: We're the elite.

MARGOT: The best of the best.

> DOLORES *hands over a document.* OLLIE *inspects it.*

DOLORES: I think my résumé speaks for itself.

ENZO: How strange.

DOLORES: I don't want to toot my own horn but I've shared the same roof with some great hermits over the years.

MARGOT: Our Oliver's one of the best hermits I know.

ENZO: World class.

DOLORES: I never realised the solitary business was so competitive.

OLLIE: It's a growth industry. This all seems to be in order.

MARGOT: But no vacancies, sorry.

ENZO: We could offer a trial period?

DOLORES: I'd be most grateful.

MARGOT: But—

ENZO: Done!

OLLIE: When can you start hermit-ing?

DOLORES: I can be on my own right away.

OLLIE: Good to have you with us.

ENZO: Or not with us.

MARGOT: As the case may be.

> DOLORES *offers her hand.* OLLIE *shakes it and is startled by a clown horn going off.*

DOLORES: Oops.

MARGOT: Oh, say it isn't so.
OLLIE: Dolores…?
DOLORES: No.

She absent-mindedly slides a red clown nose on.

MARGOT: It's the clown!
DOLORES: I panicked.
ENZO: You're back!

He embraces DOLORES.

MARGOT: Enzo!

ENZO *steps back.*

She came back to mock us.
DOLORES: I'm quite serious.

She removes her clown nose.

I want to settle down, like dust. Take up residence.
MARGOT: Were you caught in the storm?
DOLORES: I crashed again.

MARGOT *rushes to* DOLORES' *trunk, hidden away.*

ENZO: Why'd you come back, Dolores?
OLLIE: Left her shoes behind.
DOLORES: I don't need them. My feet are normal.
MARGOT: But I checked your trunk on the beach. There was nothing inside. I assumed you'd drowned.
OLLIE: [*to* MARGOT] And you didn't tell me?
DOLORES: The tides brought me back, Ollie.
ENZO: A gift from the sea.

She wipes the dust off OLLIE.

OLLIE: You ran away.
DOLORES: Did you miss me?
OLLIE: I'm a hermit. I don't miss people.
DOLORES: I want to be a recluse too.
OLLIE: You don't want that.
DOLORES: Do you?
OLLIE: I love being alone. I was just telling these two that the other day.

He departs. DOLORES *feels* MARGOT*'s stare.*

MARGOT: Enzo, make yourself scarce.

ENZO: But there's only one of me, how much more scarce can I be?

He leaves. MARGOT *points to* DOLORES*' clown shoes.*

MARGOT: Put them on and walk away. Everything has its place here, clown.

DOLORES: I'm not a clown.

She absently honks her horn. MARGOT *is startled.*

Last time, I promise.

MARGOT: I don't like that horn.

DOLORES: I can't help it.

MARGOT: Is it supposed to make me laugh?

DOLORES: It's just something to fill in the gaps.

MARGOT: I like the gaps. It's unfilled space.

DOLORES: Your whole life is a gap.

MARGOT *stares at the clown shoes.*

MARGOT: Your shoes are ridiculous.

DOLORES: Do you want to try them on?

MARGOT: Don't make me laugh.

DOLORES: Do you ever get lonely here, Margot?

MARGOT: That's the point.

DOLORES: Ah yes.

MARGOT: You don't belong.

DOLORES: I can learn.

MARGOT: You're on your own here.

DOLORES: It's the same all over.

MARGOT: There's no beg pardons.

DOLORES: Beg your pardon?

MARGOT: You know what your problem is? You're a people person.

DOLORES: I'm not.

MARGOT: You like to chat.

DOLORES: I don't.

Silence.

It's a long life to live alone.

MARGOT: If you're lucky.
DOLORES: You were lucky to find such a beautiful dress in one of the suitcases.
MARGOT: See?
DOLORES: What?
MARGOT: That's chat.
DOLORES: It is?
MARGOT: Believe me, that's chat.
DOLORES: I'm sorry.

    ENZO *eavesdrops, unnoticed.* MARGOT *goes to leave, stops.*

MARGOT: I came with it.
DOLORES: What?
MARGOT: The dress.
DOLORES: Is that chat?
MARGOT: No.
DOLORES: Oh…

    MARGOT *absently slides her foot into a clown shoe.*

Good thing you did come with it. So you could marry Enzo.
MARGOT: I'm not married to Enzo.
DOLORES: Oh… Not Ollie?
MARGOT: Louis. [*She puts on the other shoe.*] It's a familiar story…
DOLORES: Marrying a fish?
MARGOT: Happiness crashes. It's routine.
DOLORES: Where is Louis?
MARGOT: Out there, where I can't suffocate him. Where he's got a whole ocean to himself… I was told there are plenty more fish in the sea, but there's not.
DOLORES: You didn't marry a fish did you?
MARGOT: Who can say?
DOLORES: He was human?
MARGOT: 'Fish, noun, cold-blooded animal with gills'…
DOLORES: What about Enzo?
MARGOT: I don't need Enzo. I just need patience. And maybe one day, if the universe smiles on me, I'll get to see Louis the Ist crash.

    ENZO *disappears.* DOLORES *watches* MARGOT *absently walk away in the clown shoes.*

SCENE FOUR

ENZO, *in the observatory, has a razor to his neck.* DOLORES *arrives.*

ENZO: Don't come any closer!
DOLORES: What are you doing, Enzo?
ENZO: You can't stop me, Dolores.
DOLORES: Please don't hurt yourself.
ENZO: Stand back!

> *He flirts with the razor at his throat before shaving his milk moustache away.*

My moustache has reached the butter stage, time to shave it off. Because if at first you don't succeed then… you've failed.
DOLORES: What about the camembert?
ENZO: It was headed for a Danish Blue. I can't get it right, can't get anything right. You know what they say, don't you?
DOLORES: You missed a bit…
ENZO: Cheese is milk's attempt at immortality.
DOLORES: Everything has a use by date.
ENZO: [*finishing shaving*] That moustache was going to change my life.
DOLORES: It was only an idea, a little light bulb above your head. There'll be others.
ENZO: I was going to transform, transcend all this. I was going places. The world was going to be my ointment.
DOLORES: Oyster.
ENZO: I meant ointment.

> *He weeps.* DOLORES *watches on, awkwardly. Finally she puts a clown nose on him.* ENZO *is restored.*

I'm a clown?
DOLORES: Yes.
ENZO: A double act?
DOLORES: I'm afraid you're on your own, Enzo.

> *Silence.*

ENZO: I want to join the circus, Dolores. Live out of a suitcase, like you. Like all the clowns in our storeroom. I want to run away. I want to be a Bozo.

DOLORES: What about the lighthouse?
ENZO: I'm sick of the lifestyle. No-one will notice I'm gone. The big top is where I belong. The glare of the lights, the sound of the band—
DOLORES: The smell of the elephant shit.
ENZO: I can almost taste it!

SCENE FIVE

OLLIE *fills his bucket at the beach.* MARGOT, ENZO *and* DOLORES *watch.*

MARGOT: You start.
ENZO: Do I have to?
MARGOT: You know how it goes.

>OLLIE *takes sand from the beach pile to the other pile.*

ENZO: There's a lot of sand…
MARGOT: There is a lot of sand…
DOLORES: There's so much sand.

>MARGOT *and* ENZO *look at* DOLORES, *surprised.*

We've established that.

>*Silence.*

ENZO: It's a big job—
DOLORES: It is a big job—It's such a big—Point taken—And he's still got the ocean to do—He can't start that till he's got all the sand—Making progress—Coming along nicely—My word—Too right—Right you are—Yes indeed—Indeedy-do—Yes sir—Yes siree, Bob—
MARGOT: Will you stop it?! You're spoiling the routine.
DOLORES: Thought I'd free up some time.
MARGOT: What are we supposed to do with the rest of the day?

>DOLORES *gets up and moves to the beach where, unnoticed, she fills the miniature bucket.*

Now, where were we?
ENZO: Why were we?
MARGOT: You know how it goes.
ENZO: I'm struggling…
MARGOT: Don't struggle.

> OLLIE *notices* DOLORES *with her bucket, mimicking him.*

OLLIE: What are you doing?
MARGOT: What is she doing?
DOLORES: I'm helping.
OLLIE: You can't help.
MARGOT: People don't help. People are the problem.
DOLORES: This way you can finish quicker.
ENZO: 'Finish'?
OLLIE: [*continuing his task*] I don't want to finish.
DOLORES: Then why bother?
ENZO: 'Why bother'?
DOLORES: Why not just stop?
MARGOT: 'Stop'?! Come here, clown.

> DOLORES *approaches* MARGOT *and lifts up her wedding dress to reveal she is still wearing the clown shoes.*

DOLORES: You're the clown.
ENZO: [*embracing her*] Margot, we can be a duo!
MARGOT: Get them off me! [*She quickly takes off the shoes.*] It's you the circus is calling, Dolores. Back where you belong, surrounded by people and applause and feats of daring. We have no interest in such things. Do we, Enzo?
ENZO: Tell me more about the feats of daring.
MARGOT: We're very happy here. [*Calling*] Aren't we, Oliver?
OLLIE: [*calling*] Very happy.
MARGOT: We have our ways of passing the time, of—
ENZO: Margot, he's stopped stealing the beach.
MARGOT: He never stops. What's he doing?

> OLLIE, *kneeling in the sand, has discovered a human skull. The others approach.*

OLLIE: They're everywhere… The sand is riddled with them… This beach is a grave. [*He unearths more bones and skulls.*] All these bones, skeletons, skulls. All this death washed up on our shore, under our noses, under our feet… What have I done?
MARGOT: The earth is full of dead people, Oliver. All those who went before. There are more people below the ground than there are above it.

OLLIE: But the suffering we've caused…
MARGOT: They took their chances out there. They've no-one to blame but themselves.
OLLIE: We're stealing from the dead.
MARGOT: We have to live. What more can we do?
DOLORES: Isn't it obvious?

> *She looks to the observatory. The lights dim.*

MARGOT: Getting late…

> *She stares at* ENZO, *who is captivated by the skull.*

[*Pointedly*] Getting late…
ENZO: I'm a bit tired…

> *They both yawn perfunctorily.*

The sun's falling…
MARGOT: The world's turning…
ENZO: The sky's fading…
MARGOT: The darkness is coming.

> ENZO *looks resigned.* DOLORES *picks up her clown shoes forlornly.* OLLIE *drops the skull in defeat.*

OLLIE: This is the life.
ENZO: It doesn't get any better than this.
MARGOT: That was a—

> *Everyone departs, leaving* MARGOT.

… Good day.

SCENE SIX

DOLORES *places her clown shoes in the storeroom.* OLLIE *watches.*

OLLIE: Why did you come back? Was it for your package?
DOLORES: No.
OLLIE: Isn't it important?
DOLORES: Very.

> *Silence.*

Aren't you even curious about what's in it?

> OLLIE *shakes his head.* DOLORES *mimics him.*

OLLIE: Why do you copy me?

DOLORES: So you can see what you're doing.

> *She stares up at the piles of suitcases.*

So many suitcases…

OLLIE: People don't see the rocks.

DOLORES: I wonder why.

OLLIE: There are not many rocks we hit that are lit, Dolores. They're hidden. They're unexpected. That's why they get us. There's nothing I can do.

DOLORES: You could light the lamp.

OLLIE: Enzo's the caretaker.

DOLORES: It's your lighthouse.

> *Silence.*

OLLIE: Can you keep a secret?

> DOLORES *nods.*

I'm not qualified. I don't know how it works. It was abandoned. Nobody was here to show me what to do when I washed up, no instruction manual, nothing. My hands are tied.

DOLORES: These belong to other people, Ollie. They're full of cherished mementos, sentimental value. They shouldn't be here gathering dust, they shouldn't just be forgotten.

OLLIE: Better to forget than be forgotten. How do you think the piece of scrap wood used to stir a tin of paint feels when it's thrown away? Do you realise if you collected all those pieces of scrap wood and built a house out of them, then when you had to paint it the job would already be half done?

DOLORES: What are we doing here?

OLLIE: I'm stealing a beach.

DOLORES: It's pointless.

> ENZO *enters, triumphantly holding aloft a bottle.*

ENZO: Any more messages arrive for me?

OLLIE: There are never any messages.

ENZO: Look what just washed ashore.

MARGOT *appears.*

MARGOT: You got one?

DOLORES: Finally!

OLLIE: He probably sent it to himself.

DOLORES: Now what sort of person would do that? Come on, Enzo, read it.

ENZO ponders then swallows the message.

Enzo…

ENZO: It was a rejection, I could tell.

MARGOT: Quite right. You should never check incoming messages. Ollie can vouch for that.

She and OLLIE *depart.* DOLORES *presents* ENZO *with the clown shoes.*

ENZO: What are these for?

DOLORES: For running away to the circus.

ENZO: I don't want to go on my own.

DOLORES: I'm not going back, Enzo.

ENZO: Perhaps the dummy might want to go?

Silence.

DOLORES: You're not going to go are you?

ENZO: I'm definitely going. I mean there's a really good chance… It's more likely than not that I'll go… It's 50/50… 40/60… I might go.

DOLORES *takes the clown shoes and packs them into the large trunk, along with her red wig from her pocket. She takes* ENZO*'s clown nose off and throws it in.*

DOLORES: I was going to pass them on to you: my shoes, my wig, my nose…

ENZO: But—

DOLORES: But it'd be a waste. Might as well pack them away in here, where the water and salty air can't get in, and toss it out to sea. I'll do it with the first tide tomorrow.

ENZO: Don't do that.

DOLORES: Someone out there might need them.

She closes the lid on the large trunk.

ENZO: I need them.

The lights dim. Everyone settles in their suitcase beds.

[*Whispering*] Ollie...?

OLLIE: Goodnight, sleep tight, don't let the bed bugs bite.

Silence.

ENZO: Yes.

He prepares to call to MARGOT.

MARGOT: Don't even think about it!

OLLIE *creeps over to* DOLORES. *She is on her trunk, staring at her reflection in the compact mirror.*

DOLORES: The thing about clown makeup, Ollie, is you only have one face to face the world. It never cracks, never drops, it's the face everyone wants to see... I ran away to the circus the other night... again. Thought the circus missed me. But happiness goes on without you. It doesn't wait. It just goes on and you join up with it or you don't. I couldn't even do the routines anymore, simple routines, slapstick. I was missing my shoes. I was being a bad clown. Children were crying. And for the first time the circus seemed to me a sort of sad place. And my face seemed a sort of sad face.

OLLIE: You didn't fall in love with a cannonball did you?

DOLORES: I thought he was a human cannonball.

OLLIE: And he was, wasn't he?

DOLORES: All too human.

ENZO: [*whispering*] Is anyone awake? I don't want to be the last one to fall asleep.

OLLIE *starts to move back to his bed.*

DOLORES: What do you dream of, Ollie?

OLLIE: Sand, mostly. Millions of grains of sand. I'm not moving it though. At first it's nowhere to be seen. I'm standing on this empty beach. Well, not even a beach. There's no sea, no sand, only sky. I haven't stolen the sky. It's as if I've finished. I've come to the end. I'm staring at this great abyss about to swallow me up and I'm ready to surrender to it. All this time I thought when I've stolen that beach, I've won. But in my dream I haven't won. It's all gone and I look lost. I just stand there… waiting, uncertain, indifferent, at the mercy of some great unknown. And then it happens… Imperceptibly at first but building steadily to a crescendo… It's sand, Dolores. And it's raining down on me from out of the sky. I try to avoid it, to stand between the falling grains, but it's everywhere, in my hair, my eyes, my mouth, until I'm wading through it, wallowing, flailing, trying to rise above it but I have no grip and I just know this sand is going to bury me.

Silence.

DOLORES: Well, I won't ask you about your nightmares then.

They share a smile. OLLIE *rests his head on her shoulder.*

SCENE SEVEN

MARGOT *is on the beach returning sand with the bucket.*

MARGOT: [*muttering*] I'll store it under 'S' for sand or shore… 'B' for beach or bucket. There's so much sand, too much sand. We're happy here. Are we? Aren't we? You tell me.

ENZO—*dressed in clown attire and holding his ventriloquist dummy suitcase—approaches and taps* MARGOT *on the shoulder, startling her.*

ENZO: It's me.

MARGOT: What are you doing in that getup?

ENZO: I'm running away to join the circus. [*He taps his suitcase.*] So is he. We both are.

MARGOT: You're not going, Enzo.

ENZO: Oh, I'm going.

MARGOT: This is the clown's fault.

ENZO: I think I could be happy there.

MARGOT: You're happy here.

She returns sand. ENZO *follows her.*

ENZO: Contortionists, lion tamers, ringleaders—

MARGOT: Freaks, weirdos, misfits—

ENZO: Caravans, a show every night, people, music… I'm dying here.

MARGOT: We saved you. You washed up broken and bedraggled with half the ocean in your lungs.

ENZO: I fell overboard.
MARGOT: You jumped.
ENZO: We all jumped.
MARGOT: Not me, I was pushed.
ENZO: I never planned to be here. It was a pratfall, a slip on a banana peel. I just need to pick myself up and dust myself off.
MARGOT: I don't think you'll make a very good clown. You're a hermit. You've never worked with laughs.
ENZO: I'm going.
MARGOT: You don't even know how to go.
ENZO: I have a plan.

> *He turns to leave.*

MARGOT: Enzo…? I was going to give you this.

> *She hands him a hip flask.* ENZO *admires it.*

It's a hip flask… engraved…
ENZO: [*reading*] 'To My Beloved Larry, Here's cheers for 20 glorious years'… Who's Larry?
MARGOT: It's my pet name for you.
ENZO: Oh. Since when?
MARGOT: Since I found it in one of the suitcases.
ENZO: It has been a glorious twenty years, hasn't it…?

> *She nods.*

I'll treasure this. [*He sniffs the alcohol inside and recoils.*] Mind you, I don't drink.
MARGOT: You will.

> ENZO *leaves.* MARGOT *drops the bucket.*

SCENE EIGHT

OLLIE *is sleeping against* DOLORES' *shoulder as dawn breaks.* MARGOT *creeps over to the package.*

DOLORES: Uh-uh-uh, it's not yours to open.
MARGOT: I've opened everything else.
DOLORES: They weren't yours to open either.
MARGOT: No more nasty surprises. I make it my business to know.

DOLORES: Why do you need to know?
MARGOT: Because you either get wise or you get hurt. I never used to search my husband's pockets or read his diary, check his messages—it didn't even occur to me. But ignorance is a bliss that doesn't last. Better to find out first.
DOLORES: So you know what's in every suitcase?
MARGOT: It's the only way. Then I can sort through the chaos, put it in order, file it away. For instance, this one is 'T' for trinkets and treasures—

> *She opens a suitcase. Sound of discordant circus music as red helium balloons, attached to ribbon, burst out.*

Get them off me… Get them off me!

> OLLIE *awakens.*

Ollie, she put balloons in the suitcase!
OLLIE: I thought we said no more opening suitcases.
MARGOT: She opened it. She must have.
DOLORES: Maybe the balloons were already inside?
MARGOT: Who'd travel with balloons?
DOLORES: Me, for a start.
OLLIE: I think it's best if we just keep them all closed.
MARGOT: Yes, can't we be left alone together to stagnate in peace?

> DOLORES *inhales the air from a balloon.*

DOLORES: [*helium voice*] You'll never be happy.
MARGOT: We were happy… Weren't we?
OLLIE: Well…
MARGOT: Where's Enzo? He'll say we were.
DOLORES: What are you holding onto? There's nothing here.
OLLIE: Don't open that—

> DOLORES *flips open the lid on a suitcase and more red helium balloons, on ribbons, escape. Circus music swells.*

MARGOT: [*calling*] Enzo?!
DOLORES: Let it all go…

> *She flips open a trunk and more red balloons escape.*

MARGOT: Don't tell me he actually left…

DOLORES: It's just air, packaged air!

> *She flips open the lid to another case and red balloons on ribbons burst out.*

MARGOT: I don't like balloons!
OLLIE: But these were full of baggage…
DOLORES: They're empty…
OLLIE: How did you do this?
MARGOT: [*calling*] Enzo!
DOLORES: [*offering a balloon*] Care to share a balloon?

> *A curious* OLLIE *inhales the air from the balloon.*

MARGOT: Ollie, help me find him!
OLLIE: [*helium voice*] Enzo?!
MARGOT: [*calling*] Enzo?!

> *She continues her frantic search.*

OLLIE: I feel a little light-headed.
DOLORES: Then this is a good time to ask you.
OLLIE: Ask me what?
DOLORES: To come back out there, out on the high seas, with the world's most sociable hermit… with me.

> *Silence. An anxious* OLLIE *inhales from the balloon.*

Say something.
OLLIE: [*helium voice*] Um…
DOLORES: 'Um' is not going to do it for us, Ollie.
OLLIE: [*grabbing a suitcase*] Um, I'm ready.
DOLORES: What?
MARGOT: What if he left? He'll never survive out there.
OLLIE: I'm all packed.
DOLORES: To go?
OLLIE: To go.
MARGOT: Not you too? You can't swim.
DOLORES: What about the sand?
OLLIE: I didn't pack my bucket. What about the clown?
DOLORES: I'm throwing it out to sea. Look, I'll show you.

> *She flips the latch on the large trunk. It opens to reveal* ENZO, *curled up inside with the dummy, wearing the clown attire.*

MR MELANCHOLY

MARGOT stares. DOLORES *listens to his chest.*

MARGOT: Enzo…?
DOLORES: He's not breathing…
MARGOT: I told him not to go in there…
OLLIE: He needs to be resuscitated…
MARGOT: I'll do it!

She presses her lips against ENZO*'s, blowing desperately.*

Please… please…
DOLORES: I said I'd throw it out with the first tide…
MARGOT: You fool, Enzo… You buffoon, blockhead, dunce, dodo, dope, nincompoop, numskull, nitwit, chump, clod… clown! We were happy here…
OLLIE: Margot…
MARGOT: I told him there was no way out from the inside.

She pops several balloons in fury before collapsing into tears. DOLORES *looks to* OLLIE *who deliberately puts his suitcase down. Blackout.*

SCENE NINE

DOLORES *drags her trunk down to the beach. She sings the circus tune dolefully to herself.*

DOLORES: [*singing*] La da da-da la da da da
La da da-da la da da da…

OLLIE *approaches with her clown shoes.*

OLLIE: Good time to be going back out… halcyon sea.

Silence.

'Halcyon, adjective, calm or peaceful.'
DOLORES: Fancy a whole book about meaning and it leaves you with 'zucchini'…

Silence.

Did you ever take me seriously?
OLLIE: I was walking through a rough neighbourhood once, dangerous part of town. Somewhere I'd never normally be. Dark, shadowy,

broken windows, no street lights… But I was with this woman who had a black belt in martial arts, so I felt secure. We ended up getting mugged anyway because she took too long to change into her karate suit and kept trying to get this man with a flick-knife to bow—

DOLORES: Is there any point to this story?

OLLIE: The point is I would have preferred to just hand over my wallet from the outset than have a false glimmer of hope that she could save me.

DOLORES: That's your reason for staying?

OLLIE: I can't leave my post. I'm the keeper of the light.

DOLORES: Yes you are.

Silence.

OLLIE: Margot needs me.

DOLORES steps inside her trunk.

I've always taken you seriously, Dolores.

He offers her the clown shoes.

DOLORES: I'm not going back. Close the latch behind me.

She goes to pull the lid shut. OLLIE *stops her.*

OLLIE: What about your package?

DOLORES: That's yours.

OLLIE: Is it a gift?

DOLORES: No, it's yours. It's the only thing in that storeroom that is.

She pulls the lid closed on herself.

OLLIE: Goodbye…

A clown nose pokes out of a small hole in the trunk. OLLIE *picks it up and places the clown shoes down at the shore.*

For a moment there I was almost happy…

SCENE TEN

A shattered MARGOT *is on lookout at night in the observatory. She wears her black slip, folding up her wedding dress in the wind. Her arms are covered in black armbands.* OLLIE *enters the storeroom.*

MARGOT: There's a storm brewing...
OLLIE: Are you okay, Margot?
MARGOT: And a ship's due to pass tonight. Good news, isn't it?
OLLIE: You'll catch your death...
MARGOT: Where's Dolores?
OLLIE: She left.
MARGOT: Hope she doesn't crash here again...

> OLLIE *notices the package.* MARGOT *approaches.*

This is how we like it, Oliver...
OLLIE: Yes, Margot. Same. Same as it ever was.
MARGOT: Thought you'd left me...

> OLLIE *fetches the package and sits down on his suitcase.*

Dolores didn't take her package.
OLLIE: It's not hers. It's mine.

> *He opens it, staring at the contents inside. Discordant circus music creeps in.*

MARGOT: What's in it?

> OLLIE *holds up a light bulb.*

OLLIE: [*almost inaudible*] A light bulb.
MARGOT: What are you going to do?
OLLIE: [*handing her the bulb*] Put the light on, Margot.

> MARGOT *trudges up to the observatory. The circus music becomes increasingly warped.* OLLIE *stands near his bucket and the clown shoes—between the two piles of sand—uncertain.* MARGOT *puts in the new bulb and switches on the light. It works. She takes a swig from the hip flask.* OLLIE *looks out to sea at the shining light. He puts on the clown nose and stands in the clown shoes. He waves tentatively. Sand begins to rain down on him.* OLLIE *covers his head in defeat then puts his bucket on his head, like an absurd hat. A wistful smile as he stares out to sea, with the sand falling even harder. The lights fade as the strange circus music swells to a crescendo.*

THE END

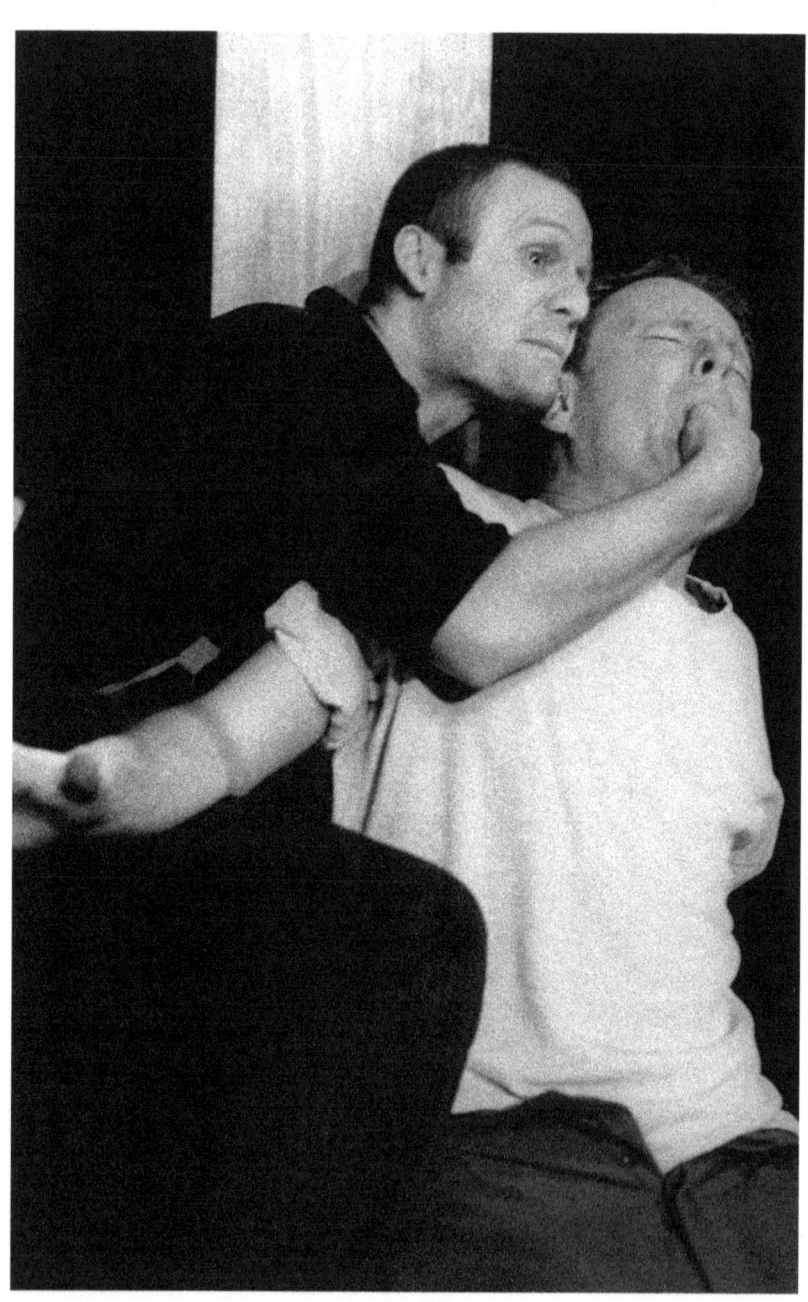

Jerome Pride as Gunther and Richard Sydenham as Errol in the 1999 Griffin Theatre Company production in Sydney. (Photo: Tracey Schramm.)

Footprints on Water

Matt Cameron

Jerome Pride as Gunther and Helen Thomson as Lena in the 1999 Griffin Theatre Company production in Sydney. (Photo: Tracey Schramm.)

Footprints on Water was first produced by La Mama on the 4 July 1997 at La Mama Theatre in Melbourne, Australia, with the following cast:

NOEL	Aidan Fennessy
EDIE	Anni Finsterer
LENA	Elise McCredie
AGNES	Christen O'Leary
GUNTHER	Jerome Pride
ERROL	Jim Russell

Director, Peter Houghton
Designer, Paul Jackson
Composer, Philippa Nihill

The author would like to thank Peter Houghton; La Mama Theatre; The British Council; Playbox Theatre Company; Chameleon Theatre; Griffin Theatre Company; and all those involved with productions, readings and workshops assisting the development of this play.

CHARACTERS
NOEL, a boot maker
EDIE, a prostitute
ERROL, a boot maker's apprentice
GUNTHER, a brothel owner
LENA, a brothel owner's wife
AGNES, a mad woman

SETTING

A timeless, placeless world. A small, rustic village near a river, protected by a levee. There is a constant sense of unrest with dogs barking and the threat of flood with heavy rains. In the village is the local brothel with its street window where the prostitute attracts clientele. Up on the hill is a church. This is Noel's house, with his still-under-construction boat, an old crate with a chessboard on it and many pairs of boots. Minorities are relegated to a rural ghetto between the river and the village—referred to as The Foreigners.

PLAYWRIGHT'S NOTE

This play lends itself to a stylised production in terms of staging and design. For instance, Noel's bike may not be actual, perhaps instead just handlebars. The foreign language in the play is fictitious. A translation is provided in the brackets at the end of each line of foreign dialogue. This language is not constructed pedantically in terms of tense or repeated prepositions and vocabulary. Key words, however, remain the same throughout. The intention is that the language be unfamiliar and uniformly generic. It should not carry a single, particular accent traceable to a known nationality. Rather, it should approach a hybrid that is, of itself, unique.

Please note: the name 'Gunther' is pronounced 'Günta'.

ACT ONE

PROLOGUE

The village. Distant sounds of dogs howling and barking in the night. All characters emerge from the shadows.

NOEL: I am Noel. I am a boot maker and Christian servant of God.
GUNTHER: I am Gunther. I am the owner of a brothel.
LENA: [*with an accent*] I am Lena. I am not a foreigner.
AGNES: I am Agnes. I am known in the village as the Sobbing Woman.
ERROL: I am Errol. I am a simple man and I am having sex with my neighbour's wife.
EDIE: I am Edie. I am, I guess, a prostitute.

SCENE ONE

The village. NOEL *is on his bike, pedalling hurriedly. He passes people calling to him in the night. A woman sobs in the distance.* ERROL *is eating from a brown paper bag full of sweets.*

ERROL: What are you doing out this time of night, Noel?
NOEL: Can't stop now, Errol.
ERROL: Do you want a lolly?

    LENA *has her shoe off and is examining the heel.*

LENA: Give me a ride home, Noel?
NOEL: Ah… sorry Mrs Lena, can't stop—No brakes.
LENA: [*waving*] Careful then.
NOEL: It's mostly uphill… [*He mutters.*] Do I have to run into everyone I know?

    AGNES *appears with her wooden bucket full of water.*

AGNES: The river is getting lower, Noel.
NOEL: Don't speak to me.

    He pedals on as GUNTHER *steps forward with a limp.*

GUNTHER: Been to Red Light House, Noel?

NOEL: Heavens, no. Just getting some fresh air.
GUNTHER: You sly dog…
NOEL: Please Gunther, you must read the Good Book.

> *He tosses* GUNTHER *a small Bible and pedals away furiously.*

GUNTHER: [*calling*] Hope my Edie looked after you.

> NOEL *looks back to see* EDIE *under the brothel window's red light. She stares at* NOEL.

EDIE: Why do you keep coming here? When you look at me, look me in the eye. Look me in the eye. Look me in the eye. Look me in the eye—
NOEL: Don't look her in the eye.

> *He pedals on alone in the night.*

Keep your eyes firmly fixed on the Lord. Oh God, forgive me.

> *Blackout.*

SCENE TWO

The church. ERROL, *working on a pile of boots, whistles.* NOEL *appears, carrying his Bible. He is short of breath and perspiring from the fierce sun outside.*

NOEL: This Godless place. Sunday… His day and—Stop whistling!

> ERROL *continues whistling.*

Do you have to be so… chipper? It's depressing. One day, Errol. Those heathen souls down there can't even pretend to be pure of thought for the Lord's day—Will you stop, you imbecile! Use your tongue.
ERROL: I can whistle.
NOEL: [*to the heavens*] He talks! They're praying across the valley, you know. I heard the convent bells on the breeze. Did you hear them?

> ERROL *shakes his head.*

This village used to come up here… every Sunday…
ERROL: The foreigners too?
NOEL: God, no.

ERROL *resumes whistling.*

I built this church to please Him. To bring His people within reach of His ear, to whisper our goodness, to serenade Him with hymns. I even built a steeple, a finger pointing up to God.

ERROL *clasps his hands together, performing a childish rhyme.*

ERROL: 'Here's the church, here's the steeple, open the doors, see all the people.'

NOEL: There are no people. God got distracted when He made you, didn't He? There was a knock at the door or the phone rang... and you never got finished... Mysterious ways... That hill will be the death of me.

ERROL: Why do you live up here?

NOEL: They all used to come to me... To confide, to confess...

ERROL: You complain about the hill everyday. Every time you come back, 'The hill's steep, Errol'... I know that. It's a hill, Noel. Hills go up.

NOEL: Yes, hills go up. Good, Errol.

ERROL: And hills go down again on the other side. They go up and they go down—

NOEL: The point, Errol, is that this one's getting steeper...

ERROL: Hills go up, hills go down. Hills go up—

NOEL: It's quite noticeable. Each day it's becoming harder to climb.

ERROL: I don't know why you stay up here.

NOEL: Closer to God.

ERROL: What's he ever done? I never see him around.

NOEL: The Lord moves in mysterious ways.

ERROL: Can't he walk normally?

NOEL *shakes his head in disbelief.*

Come and live down in the village, Noel.

He starts whistling again.

NOEL: The village? Stop that!

ERROL *stops whistling. He selects from his bag of sweets.*

It's a cesspool down there.

ERROL: I live down there. We all live down there.

NOEL: Except me. It's a pigsty.
ERROL: It's not. Maybe out with the foreigners, but not in our part of the village it's not. Christ, I mean—
NOEL: The Lord's name.
ERROL: What?
NOEL: The Lord's name.

He taps his Bible.

ERROL: Isn't it 'God'?
NOEL: How many times have I told you this? Don't curse using the name of the Almighty.
ERROL: Like that time I hit my thumb? And I shouted out 'Jesus'?
NOEL: Don't take it in vain, you wouldn't like it.
ERROL: Do you think God hits his thumb and shouts 'Errol'?
NOEL: God wouldn't curse. And God wouldn't even know who you are.
ERROL: He probably doesn't even have thumbs. Do you want a lolly?
NOEL: They'll rot your teeth. Of course He has thumbs. How do you think He made everything?
ERROL: [*chewing*] These are good ones… Gunther says he saw you at Red Light House last night.
NOEL: That's a lie. I may have ridden past…
ERROL: But did you go for a ride inside?

NOEL slaps ERROL's grinning face.

NOEL: I don't want that gutter talk in my church.
ERROL: [*holding his face*] Gunther said it. He saw you at Red Light House. It wasn't me.
NOEL: Don't you listen to him. He'll fill your head with serpents… I used to think the women in that place were so friendly…

The brothel. Red light on EDIE. She makes a provocative gesture to potential clients.

Tapping on the window to invite me in for a game of Backgammon…
ERROL: Backgammon?

NOEL makes a shaking the dice motion.

NOEL: I thought this was shaking the dice. Soon found out they were just whores.

Red light down on EDIE.

ERROL: [*nodding*] Just whores, they're just whores, Noel… Just whores… I like Edie. She smells good.

NOEL: You sinners stick together.

ERROL: I don't go there anymore.

NOEL: Got yourself a free harlot?

ERROL: Edie says you think you're holier than thou.

NOEL: If thou is everyone in this village… yes.

ERROL: She says that sitting up top of a hill doesn't make you closer to God—

NOEL: I can speak in tongues, Errol.

He hits ERROL *repeatedly on the head with his Bible.*

You tell your jezebel that. I have a direct line to the Lord. I know his language. 'Blessed are those who fear the Lord and walk in his ways.'

ERROL *suddenly grabs* NOEL *with brute strength.*

ERROL: If you hit me again, I'll… I'll… I will! Don't think I won't!

NOEL: Do you want a game of chess?

ERROL: Yes please.

NOEL *and* ERROL *sit at the chess board crate. Several pieces are missing. They have been replaced with sundry items: spice bottles etc. They place the pieces with certainty.*

NOEL & ERROL: 'The salt is my queen, the spice is my knight, the glue is my king, the vanilla essence is my pawn'—

ERROL: What's the bishop?

NOEL: The bishop.

He holds up the actual chess piece. They finish setting the board.
ERROL *holds salt and pepper shakers behind his back.*

ERROL: Which hand?

NOEL: Right.

ERROL *shows the pepper shaker in his right hand.*

ERROL: Pepper. I'm on salt.

They switch sides and ponder the board. ERROL *takes a long time, changing his mind about moving the vanilla essence.*

NOEL: There's a use by date on that.
ERROL: Ssh… I'm thinking…
NOEL: We do have to make some boots today. And I've got to work on my boat.

> ERROL *moves but keeps a finger on the piece.* NOEL *moves.*

ERROL: Uh-uh-uh…

> *He points at his finger, moves the piece back then moves another pawn.*

Can pawn take queen?
NOEL: Very rare. Don't even think of it, you're too slow.
ERROL: [*releasing his finger*] Your move.

> NOEL *moves swiftly.*

NOEL: Your move.
ERROL: Do you believe in [*mispronouncing*] Buddhism, Noel?
NOEL: [*correcting*] 'Buddhism' and there is only one Lord and Saviour and he's not a bald, fat Indian. [*He moves.*] Your move.

> *They continue playing chess.*

ERROL: I've been reading about it.
NOEL: There's only one book—the Good Book, with Testaments two, Old and New—and don't lie to me, you can't read.
ERROL: Edie's been reading it to me.
NOEL: What are you doing letting a prostitute read to you?
ERROL: In this book it says that…

> *The brothel. Red light on* EDIE.

EDIE: 'Human existence is pain, Errol, caused by desire'.

> *Red light down on* EDIE.

ERROL: 'Desire'…
NOEL: Desire is for the weak.
ERROL: This book, about Zen, it's got a problem in it.
NOEL: There's more than one problem with Zen.
ERROL: It's a puzzle. A man puts a baby duck inside a bottle.
NOEL: Which man? Who?
ERROL: A man. I don't know his name.
NOEL: Whoever it is, it's a pointless thing to be doing.

ERROL: Can I finish my story?
NOEL: The duck turns into a swan and it's beautiful, I've heard it.
ERROL: The duck grows. So the man can't get it back out the neck of the bottle.
NOEL: Your move.
ERROL: Yes, but what can he do?
NOEL: Apologise to the duck?
ERROL: No.
NOEL: Break the bottle?
ERROL: I guessed that.
NOEL: Oh good.
ERROL: But it's not allowed. That's the puzzle, Edie says. How to get the duck out without breaking the bottle or harming the duck?
NOEL: Can't be done.
ERROL: Can't be done.
NOEL: It's unsolvable.
ERROL: Can't be done. That's what I said.
NOEL: If the duck hadn't grown…
ERROL: That's what I said.
NOEL: Oh good, great minds… Your move.
ERROL: But Edie said…

The brothel. Red light on EDIE.

EDIE: You can't undo what has been done, Errol. Each action leads to another, not the same in reverse.

Red light down on EDIE.

NOEL: What do I care? It's the duck's problem.
ERROL: If a man… has sex with his friend's wife—?
NOEL: It's a sin.
ERROL: Can the sin be—?
NOEL: What's done is done.
ERROL: Can it be undone?
NOEL: It's an unforgivable sin worthy of the wrath of God and an eternity in the pit of hell. Why?
ERROL: No reason.

Silence.

NOEL: How is Gunther?

ERROL *nervously knocks over a chess piece.*

SCENE THREE

The brothel. EDIE *is knitting in the brothel window.* GUNTHER, *wiping the sweat with a cloth, limps in with the sole of his shoe flapping.*

EDIE: Losing your sole, Gunther?
GUNTHER: Is that supposed to be clever?
EDIE: Why, don't you get it?
GUNTHER: This heat... Hell, it's like living in a furnace.

He takes off the boot and watches her knit.

Haven't we spoken about this?
EDIE: What?
GUNTHER: This... knitting.
EDIE: On a craft level?
GUNTHER: Look around. This is an establishment.
EDIE: A whorehouse.
GUNTHER: You are an advertisement for it. Men see you and they come in or they don't come in. For example, I'm a customer and I see you through the window, knitting. I'm not thinking sex, I'm thinking Grandma.
EDIE: Do I look like a grandma?

GUNTHER *removes his sock to look at his bandaged foot.*

GUNTHER: Dirty dogs... they're feral. Just attacked me...
EDIE: After you kicked them.
GUNTHER: They were going to attack me.
EDIE: What were you doing out in The Foreigners?
GUNTHER: Not one of them called their dogs off. I don't think they feed them. They're always barking. And the way they went after my foot, you'd swear I was a piece of meat.
EDIE: Try sitting in this window all day. Are you going to pay me? I haven't been paid.

GUNTHER *touches his wounded foot.*

GUNTHER: Feet...

EDIE: You're going to get all philosophical, aren't you?
GUNTHER: Where human experience begins, Edie.
EDIE: I knew it.
GUNTHER: We make contact with the ground... Feet connect us to where we stand, where we want to be. They leave a mark to show where we've been. A trail to where we've gone... I surprise you, don't I?
EDIE: You are a poet, Gunther.
GUNTHER: Mind your tongue. A little respect...
EDIE: With those socks?
GUNTHER: What's wrong with these socks?
EDIE: Do you want me to knit you some?
GUNTHER: See, your trail stops here, Edie. I don't know where they came from but your footprints lead to here.
EDIE: I can go any time.
GUNTHER: You shouldn't need to say that. I ought to go up to Noel's and get this repaired. [*He winces.*] That tongue's chafing... Those dogs will pay.
EDIE: Are you going to pay?
GUNTHER: No.
EDIE: You said you'd pay me.
GUNTHER: No, I said—
EDIE: You said you'd pay me today—
GUNTHER: If you let me finish! [*He checks his temper.*] You haven't been charging the foreigners extra. It's policy.
EDIE: But Gunther—
GUNTHER: I am a fair man, Edie.
EDIE: You shouldn't need to say that.

GUNTHER takes out a blade. He slices out the shoe's tongue.

GUNTHER: I allow those foreigners on my premises, why not. But my girls expect more for doing a foreigner. I'm a businessman, so I charge extra. You've been returning the extra to our foreign clientele. My girls want their extra pay. I have to make up the difference. So I lose. Money. My reputation. My temper. Never think that I don't know what's going on. Tongues will wag...

He waves the shoe tongue at her, smiling. He throws it away.

If it causes discomfort, get rid of it. You're new here, so I'll cut you some slack. I don't know where you came from but—

EDIE: It doesn't matter.

GUNTHER: As long as my customers are satisfied.

EDIE: I'm not a charity.

GUNTHER: And I'm not a fool.

EDIE: If you're going to screw me, Gunther, you need to pay for it.

GUNTHER: I never pay for it. I have a wife.

He leaves.

SCENE FOUR

The village. LENA *is filing her fingernails, watching* AGNES *pour the water from her bucket down the well.*

AGNES: Another load, Lena.

LENA: Nobody care. Can you not see that?

AGNES: I'm getting somewhere now.

LENA: Nobody is hearing what you say.

AGNES: The elements are gathering in my favour, the drought, the heat… Everything is cracking.

LENA: Gunther don't want you here, in village. Bad for business.

AGNES: It's a public place.

LENA: You can tip water anywhere. The well is near business, it has water, leave it. *Yip dettay, yip dettay.* [Go away.]

AGNES: Do you think there's enough room down there?

LENA: Don't come here. Gunther say stay away.

AGNES: Did he tell you to tell me this?

LENA: *Zige.* [Yes.]

AGNES: I don't believe you. You don't do what he tells you.

LENA: You upset customers.

AGNES: No, I upset you, Lena.

LENA: You not belong here.

AGNES: You're the foreigner. Don't be fooled because nobody mentions it. They know. Every time you open your mouth. And there's not enough soap to wash away how you smell. Gunther's perfume can't hide it. Don't think for a moment the animals here can't smell a foreigner in their midst.

LENA: It you they turn their noses at, not me.
AGNES: If it weren't for Gunther, you'd be living with your own out there by the levee. That's why you chose him, why else? No-one dares say anything to him.
LENA: Nothing to say. Nobody question.
AGNES: Because it's Gunther.

Silence.

Does he hurt you?
LENA: I beat him up. Can you believe that? He heavy sleeper... I punch him in the face when he sound asleep... [*She punches.*] *Uke, dunom, baste.* [One, two, three.] *Puchte, zelmana lokdo kipe stuhito, gervay, oay dupde!* [Punch, take that you pig, you stupid dog.] My hand get sore... He just lie, twitching like it mosquito... I might [*punching*] *puchte* [punch] him in the back tonight if he give me trouble.
AGNES: Doesn't he know?
LENA: He think it him. I tell him he restless sleeper. Never could believe I dare to do it... But when it dark, *puchte* [punch]... little justice.
AGNES: Little justices are not enough.
LENA: Noel say you can no judge until you walk in someone shoes.
AGNES: He's a dangerous man.
LENA: He good man. *Upe manake religiso.* [A religious man.] *Upe manake ofto Godavay.* [A man of God.]
AGNES: I wasn't judging you...
LENA: You no right to judge anyone.
AGNES: I know your kind. You'll never be loved, Lena. You've turned your back on the only people who will ever have you.
LENA: Everyone hate you. You dirt, no more than dirt. They hate you for what you do.
AGNES: I don't need to be loved, whore.
LENA: Ooh, mad woman! Mad woman! Mad woman!
AGNES: I have my bucket and my job to do and I'll have my moment. Not long now.
LENA: *Mae duotey nat-vikity. Hew bique, hew bique, sobat, sobat, elvey sobat.* [You fool no-one. Every night, every night, sobbing, sobbing, always sobbing.]

AGNES: *Lingdeta, nat, lingdeta. Mektavag piqdi, sobat elbat nay vo. Eke... ah... lorg doatoe, tiertay. Piq piteato tiertay.* [Never, no, never. I hear the sobbing at night too but I don't know where the tears come from. They are not my tears.]
LENA: They your tears. You sob, keep us wake, always never sleep. I hear you, I hear you, in my head. *Sobat, sobat, elvey sobat.* [Sobbing, sobbing, always sobbing.]
AGNES: I am known in the village as the Sobbing Woman but they're not my tears.
LENA: You cry. You cry for your past.
AGNES: I am very happy, Lena. My moment is coming.
LENA: Stay away. Please, stay away.
AGNES: He still asks after you.
LENA: Who?
AGNES: You know who. He's looking for you.
LENA: He no speak to you. Nobody speak to you.

>   *She leaves.*

SCENE FIVE

The church. NOEL *and* ERROL *are still playing chess.*

NOEL: Checkmate.
ERROL: That's not my king. That's a castle.
NOEL: You said the seasoning was your rook.
ERROL: The herbs, not the garlic.
NOEL: You don't know which is which, you can't even read. Cheat! You are a cheat! The Lord is watching. You should know it's wrong.
ERROL: It's only a game, Noel.
NOEL: So why cheat?

>   LENA *enters.*

LENA: *Gerstut deka tortepe.* [Good day gentlemen.] Is this bad time?
NOEL: I was just telling Errol that it's a sin to cheat. Don't you agree, Mrs Lena?
LENA: I need boot fix. Errol say he would do.

>   *She holds her foot up for* ERROL *to examine.*

NOEL: Is Gunther happy with his shoes, Mrs Lena?
LENA: Gunther say his sole coming... ah, off... loose.
NOEL: It's a common problem in the village. Must be the terrain.
ERROL: [*to* NOEL] I can fix this.
NOEL: Perhaps Mrs Lena would prefer someone who doesn't cheat?
LENA: No, Noel, you busy.

> NOEL *turns away to grab a hammer.* LENA *puts her hand on* ERROL's *groin.*

NOEL: Never too busy to do my handiwork.
ERROL: Let me do it, Noel.
LENA: Let Errol do it.
NOEL: You prefer an apprentice? Well... at your own peril. I only took him in out of the goodness of my heart. His knowledge of the craft is negligible and my piety has cost me business but you're the customer so... I guess I'll ride down to the village. Sunday, Mrs Lena, and no church. It's unthinkable, isn't it?
LENA: Mmm...
NOEL: Well, if Mohammad won't go to the mountain, then the mountain must go to Mohammad. I shall take the scriptures to the streets. You'll think of what I said about cheating, Errol?
ERROL: It's only a game of chess, Noel.
NOEL: God sees all.
ERROL: Yes.
NOEL: Keep your eyes firmly fixed on the Lord.

> *He gets on his bike, rings the bell and pedals.* ERROL *watches* NOEL *ride away.*

LENA: Gone?

> ERROL *nods nervously. He examines her boot.*

ERROL: It looks like the heel...
LENA: No talk.
ERROL: I don't know what to do...
LENA: Still?

> *She puts her foot on his shoulder, revealing her leg.* ERROL *removes her boot and sniffs it lustily. He tosses it away. He peels off her sock, flexes it and jams it into his underwear.*

Pusei perditay harvaka es ankum manake. [You are a very beautiful man.]

She removes his belt. ERROL *pauses, mid-arousal.*

ERROL: Is that good?
LENA: *Zige.* [Yes.]

ERROL *stands with* LENA *straddling him. His pants fall.*

ERROL: I've got my lucky underwear on.
LENA: Not for long.

ERROL *shuffles, looking for something to lie down on. He puts her down and steps back, ceasing the passion.*

ERROL: Lena, I think we should, ah… pause… before this starts getting… sexual.

Silence. ERROL *starts doing up his pants.*

LENA: Is that long enough pause?
ERROL: Yes.

He drops his pants and rushes to her. They progress quickly towards intercourse. LENA *takes all the initiative.*

The village. NOEL, *pedalling faster on his bike.*

The church. LENA *and* ERROL *are having loud and primal sex;* LENA *is on all fours.*

LENA: *Zige, zige, zige.* [Yes.] *Vixti!* [Good.] *Pre portei!* [Faster.] *Vixti! Zige!*
ERROL: *Vixti! Zige!*

NOEL *pedals furiously, venting his frustrations and ringing his bell at their moment of climax.*

LENA: *Zige, zige!*
ERROL: *Zige, zige!*

NOEL *stops pedalling and cruises.* LENA *and* ERROL *are heaving, post-coital on the floor.*

What we're doing is wrong, Lena.
LENA: No, I think we getting better.

SCENE SIX

The village. NOEL *rides his bike, clutching his Bible.*

NOEL: 'When the Lord saw how wicked everyone on earth was and how evil their thoughts were all the time, he was sorry he had ever made them and put them on the earth.' Genesis 6, verse 5. This village is sick to the core, Lord. Morally diseased. Depraved. Too far gone to be saved. Prostitutes, pagans, adulterers and cheats. Time to wipe the slate clean and start anew. If it is weakness of the flesh they desire dear God, then deliver. Bring on a bubonic plague. Fill these grimy streets with pestilence. Cover them all with weeping sores, boils and bulbous cysts.

The brothel. Red light on the street window. EDIE *is not there.*

Gone? Have you claimed the harlot already Lord? I might have said something to her, a last rite perhaps, a kind word, a forgiving word… I might have even looked her in the eye.

SCENE SEVEN

The brothel. GUNTHER *watches* EDIE *putting makeup on. He wipes the sweat from his neck with a cloth.*

GUNTHER: Look me in the eye.
EDIE: I told you, I haven't seen her, Gunther. She's your wife. Don't you know what she gets up to?
GUNTHER: She doesn't get up to anything.
EDIE: Can I go now?
GUNTHER: Don't be scared of me. You're my girl. I know about you.
EDIE: What do you know?
GUNTHER: I know what you do back here. Or more to the point, what you don't do.
EDIE: I can do this job, Gunther.
GUNTHER: I've had complaints.
EDIE: Don't get rid of me. I can be good.
GUNTHER: A 'good' girl?
EDIE: I came here to be good.
GUNTHER: In a whorehouse?

EDIE: I came here to see the world. To really see it.
GUNTHER: Where have you run from?
EDIE: You don't want to know.
GUNTHER: You can't work in my brothel and not have sex.
EDIE: There are other possibilities. It just requires a little imagination…

> GUNTHER *stares at her.*

GUNTHER: Lick me. Lick my face…

> EDIE *licks his face.* GUNTHER *closes his eyes.*

Keep licking…
EDIE: Yes. That's it. Demean me, Gunther. Take me down…
GUNTHER: 'Take you down'?
EDIE: To the depths. I want to see the darkness.
GUNTHER: Is this what my customers pay you for? This talk?
EDIE: Whatever they want. I fulfil their perverse desires…
GUNTHER: They want sex.
EDIE: They can get that from the other girls.
GUNTHER: Keep licking… I've never had a virgin prostitute working here before.
EDIE: Take me down to where you live.
GUNTHER: 'Where I live'?
EDIE: To the darkness…

> GUNTHER *suddenly covers her head with his cloth and pulls it taut around her face.*

GUNTHER: 'The darkness'?
EDIE: To the depths…
GUNTHER: 'The depths'?
EDIE: Take me down… Open my eyes…
GUNTHER: You're not afraid of the dark?
EDIE: Take me there…
GUNTHER: To where the dogs are howling?
EDIE: Yes…
GUNTHER: Down into the fury?
EDIE: Yes…
GUNTHER: Where you sell your soul for some silence?
EDIE: Yes…

GUNTHER *releases the cloth from around her face.*

GUNTHER: Do you really want me inside you?
EDIE: What do you mean?
GUNTHER: Don't play with me. Keep licking.

EDIE *licks his face.*

EDIE: Come on… You can do better…
GUNTHER: I want you to pant for me.
EDIE: What?
GUNTHER: Pant. [*He breathes in and out heavily.*] Pant! Do it!

EDIE *pants.*

Animals pant… We used to have each other like animals. Against walls, embedding our bodies into stone… bruised, cut, sweating into each other's pores, tearing each other's skins off to escape inside…

EDIE: Doesn't your wife want you anymore?
GUNTHER: My wife worships me.
EDIE: Take me all the way down.
GUNTHER: Not yet. What do my customers get from you?
EDIE: They get what they need.
GUNTHER: What do they get?
EDIE: They get unburdened. Then they get held. Do you want that?

GUNTHER *runs his hand down* EDIE*'s body.*

GUNTHER: 'Wish upon my lips. Lust into my eyes. In my sweet heart, dark desire lies.'
EDIE: What is that?
GUNTHER: It's what she said to me. The woman of the night who gave me my manhood. I can still see her in her red lit window. Eyes only for me. All flesh and fantasy. Promising me everything.
EDIE: I don't do everything, Gunther.
GUNTHER: Then you better make sure you do everything else. Things you never even thought of. Let them take you down.
EDIE: I want to see what's underneath.
GUNTHER: And you will, Edie. Trust me. Whatever is hidden is always found in the back room. This is the place where secrets get out.

SCENE EIGHT

The village. Night. NOEL *preaches to the empty streets in the mist. The distant dogs bark and howl.*

NOEL: How deaf are those who refuse the word of the Lord. The devil's hand is warm but it never lets go. And who among us can pray with one hand? God is calling you…

> AGNES *appears, straining with a bucket load.*

AGNES: Another load, Noel.
NOEL: Not you, Agnes. [*He calls to the streets.*] He's not calling all of you, but some. You should know who you are. Be wise and repent. The end is at hand. All that you know will be level with the ground. These are your last days.
AGNES: You said that last year.
NOEL: Go away.

> AGNES *retreats to the shadows.* NOEL *calls to the streets.*

Once I was blind, now I can see. Once I was deaf, now I can hear. Once I was mute, now— [*He chokes*] I just swallowed a fly. See how dirty these streets are? They are infected, infested. Armageddon is descending. You cannot afford ignorance and denial. Matthew 23, Ezekiel 38 and 39…

> EDIE *emerges.*

EDIE: What's all the shouting?

> NOEL *looks at* EDIE*'s feet.*

Is there something particularly interesting about my feet? I'm up here. Who were you shouting at?
NOEL: I'm trying to wake up His people.
EDIE: They're awake now. Who is this for?

> NOEL *motions with his head to the sky.*

What is that, a tic?
NOEL: God.
EDIE: Ah…
NOEL: I'm the only one in the village. The only man of faith. The only man of God. I don't want to be seen here.

EDIE: Then you should stop riding past every night. What is it you want? Prices?
NOEL: No… please…
EDIE: Can't you look a woman in the eye?
NOEL: You're a fallen woman.
EDIE: Yes, we keep all the fallen men company.
NOEL: I'm not a fallen man.
EDIE: Have you got an erection?
NOEL: [*gulping*] Hmm?
EDIE: Do I make you uncomfortable? Or is it just God?

Silence.

The mist is coming in…
NOEL: Every night. As soon as the dogs start up, the fog creeps in from The Foreigners… Some think it's their spirits…
EDIE: Gunther says it's their stench.
NOEL: Does he hurt you?
EDIE: I can handle his kind. What do you care?
NOEL: I don't… They're good quality boots. Keep the water out.
EDIE: It hasn't rained for ages. These are for show. Too small. They give me blisters.
NOEL: Boils?
EDIE: No.
NOEL: There's a plague on its way.
EDIE: You want me and you don't know what to do about it, do you?
NOEL: Actually, everyone's going to get sick and die. Pestilence.
EDIE: Pestilence?
NOEL: A really bad flu at least.
EDIE: Desire's making a mess of you, isn't it?
NOEL: Desire is for the weak.
EDIE: But isn't it you I see, late at night? Watching men come and go, full of envy?
NOEL: [*reading from his Bible*] 'Do not be envious of sinful people, let reverence for the Lord be the concern of your life.' Proverbs 23, verse 17.
EDIE: Does that help?

NOEL: I don't like what you do. God doesn't like what you do. My only interest here is to save you from evil. To save your soul.
EDIE: You are a boot maker…
NOEL: I am a boot maker and a Christian Servant of God…
EDIE: Soles are your area of expertise…
NOEL: That is if your soul is not already beyond absolution because you betray the very sanctity—
EDIE: Is this foreplay for you?

> AGNES *has been eavesdropping in the shadows.*

AGNES: Still no rain.

> EDIE *and* NOEL *are startled.*

I want to borrow some glue, Noel, for my bucket. I only need a small amount then I can keep up my work.
NOEL: I can't help you.
AGNES: You make boots, you must have glue. I could come up and fetch it?
NOEL: You have no place at the top of my hill. I don't want your kind up there.
AGNES: I am your kind, Noel.
NOEL: Not anymore.
AGNES: There's no point building your boat. The river is getting lower. It's getting lower.
EDIE: We need some rain, Agnes…
AGNES: No!

> *She hurries away.*

EDIE: You treat her like she's got the plague.
NOEL: She will have soon. [*He calls after her.*] She'll be the first!
EDIE: Worse than me?
NOEL: Your turn will come. All of you here at… Satan's boudoir.
EDIE: Very tense, aren't you?
NOEL: I like to be tense.
EDIE: You need a massage.
NOEL: There's too much relaxing goes on in this Godless place. Loose muscles, loose morals.
EDIE: Does Agnes have loose morals?

NOEL: She has no place here.
EDIE: Nobody will ever tell me what she's doing… with the bucket. She passes this window all day, every day. I watch her, bringing water to the well. Why? Why won't anyone say what she's doing?
NOEL: She's emptying the river.

SCENE NINE

The church. LENA *and* ERROL *finish dressing.*

ERROL: Noel will be back soon. Will I see you again, Lena?
LENA: Close your eyes, Errol…

> *She covers* ERROL's *eyes then uncovers them.*

Open. There, you see me again. You asked that last time. Look what happen.

> ERROL *takes out some coins from his pocket.*

ERROL: I should pay you. Definitely this time.
LENA: Put away.
ERROL: Why don't I pay?
LENA: I not whore, Errol. No money.
ERROL: I always pay Edie.
LENA: This different.
ERROL: This is really different.
LENA: Don't pay me.
ERROL: Gunther will be mad if I don't pay.
LENA: That would be worse. I not one of his girls.
ERROL: You won't tell him I didn't pay?
LENA: Promise.
ERROL: Because I've tried to pay. I've tried to do the right thing.
LENA: It our little secret.

> ERROL *goes to kiss* LENA *but she pulls away.*

Enough for now.
ERROL: I love you.
LENA: We can keep doing this without you saying that. You no say that to a whore, do you?

> *He nods. She kisses his forehead.*

ERROL: Noel says it's a sin to do this. Says I'll go to hell. Will you?
LENA: You not be lonely there.
ERROL: When's our next time?
LENA: [*shrugging*] When I feel like it.

    NOEL *arrives, noticing that* LENA *is missing one boot.*

NOEL: How's your 'boot fix', Mrs Lena? Must need a lot of fixing or perhaps Errol is just not very good at his work?
LENA: We just finished.
NOEL: I've been gone a long time.
ERROL: I fixed her boot, Noel. It… It was the… heel.
NOEL: Good. Where is it?
LENA: Over there, Errol.

    ERROL *fetches the strewn boot.* LENA *puts it on.*

NOEL: Do you always throw the boot away after fixing it?
LENA: He testing. It strong.
NOEL: The thing is I'm quite sure it was the other boot that you said needed repair.

    Silence.

LENA: He fix both boot!
ERROL: I fix both boot, Noel!
LENA: Thank you, Errol.
ERROL: My pleasure.
NOEL: I'm sure it was.
LENA: How much I owe you?
ERROL: Don't pay me.
NOEL: We don't charge for that particular service here, Mrs Lena. Be careful out. It's dark and the mist is especially thick tonight.
ERROL: I should go with her.
NOEL: You should clean up.
LENA: I go now. *Gerstut nakta tortepe.* [Good night gentlemen.]

    She leaves.

NOEL: [*calling*] Take care, there's a plague on it's way. This is not Red Light House, Errol! Several clues. Lack of prostitutes is one! Up here of all places, right under the nose of God. Not long before I

sail away from this God forsaken place. Finish my boat and find somewhere where the people are honest and hardworking. Good, moral, God-fearing people.
ERROL: Are you afraid of God, Noel?
NOEL: Well, yes, but in a good way.
ERROL: What's good about it?
NOEL: Stops me from having impure... desires.
ERROL: 'Human existence is pain caused by desire'. That's what that book Edie reads me says.
NOEL: I don't pay you enough for that many visits.
ERROL: Is desire the same as love?
NOEL: You read one book and you go on and on about it, don't you? Take it as doctrine, treat it as gospel and you can't even read. The harlot probably made it all up.
ERROL: Is desire the same as love?
NOEL: Desire is sub-human. We're not animals, Errol. We can control our needs... quell them. Repression is what separates man from beast. There's a lot to be said for repression.
ERROL: I need help.
NOEL: Look to the Lord.
ERROL: But I need real help. I can't sleep.
NOEL: The guilty never sleep.
ERROL: It's all this sex.
NOEL: Shush now.
ERROL: I don't know what to. Can't you tell me what to do?

    NOEL *busies himself with the boat.*

What should I feel?
NOEL: You could start with ashamed.
ERROL: It's all secret, all the time, I don't know what I can say to anyone.
NOEL: I can't hear you.
ERROL: She won't hold me, she doesn't like to kiss.
NOEL: Edie?
ERROL: No, Lena.
NOEL: [*covering his ears*] I definitely can't hear you.
ERROL: She talks dirty. Do they all do that?

NOEL: [*ignoring*] I'm sorry, is there someone here?
ERROL: And what if I love her?
NOEL: I can't hear anything!
ERROL: Can't you tell me what to do?
NOEL: Pray!
ERROL: Don't you know what to do?
NOEL: Yes, go down into the village and see if the apocalypse has arrived. You are banished from here! Exiled! You have no place in this church. In this most sacred of places, at the top of my hill, under the eyes of God. Get out of His sight!

Silence.

ERROL: I thought you could help me.

He leaves.

SCENE TEN

The Foreigners. The river and the dogs are close. A lost LENA *encounters* AGNES *in the mist.*

AGNES: Have you come to see him, Lena?
LENA: I lost. Tell me which is way to Red Light House. Gunther will be waiting.
AGNES: You don't belong there. You don't even know the way.
LENA: The mist so thick tonight.
AGNES: I'll collect my load from the river then I can walk you back.
LENA: Just tell me which is way, Agnes.
AGNES: Strange that you should end up at The Foreigners when you're lost… instinct perhaps.
LENA: I want to go home.
AGNES: You are. He wants to see you. You owe him that.
LENA: I am not a foreigner.

Sound of dogs barking.

AGNES: They're very restless tonight. Something's got their hackles up. [*She sniffs.*] What's that smell?
LENA: Gunther.

GUNTHER *appears, carrying a handful of raw meat. Sound of low growling.*

GUNTHER: What are you doing out here?

LENA: I lost.

GUNTHER: You're not meant to be here.

LENA: I could not see in fog. Don't let them see you, Gunther.

GUNTHER: I haven't seen you all day, Lena. Don't hang around here. People will think I married a foreigner.

He kisses her gently.

I've been looking for you.

LENA: *Gerstut* [Good].

GUNTHER: English.

LENA: Sorry, good.

GUNTHER: When are you going to stop doing that? You know I don't like to hear that talk.

LENA: Don't be anger.

GUNTHER: 'Angry'. Aren't you practising? You give yourself away every time you speak.

LENA: I practice.

GUNTHER: God, it stinks here… [*To the dogs*] You want to try again? Look at the mangy mongrels… I have some dinner for you mutts!

AGNES: What's in it?

GUNTHER: Glass. Rip them up inside before they even realised.

He goes to throw the bundle of meat but LENA *grabs him and kisses him passionately.*

LENA: Can you take me home, Gunther?

GUNTHER: Remember this foot, you dirty dogs.

AGNES: I hope you find your way, Lena.

LENA *and* GUNTHER *leave.*

Don't want to be left walking out here day and night. It's no place to be. I have a job to do. It's different for me… It's different. When I've cleared the river, then I'll have a home. I'll lie down on the bed of the river and I'll have earned my rest.

She sobs, wailing through the night. Sound of dogs howling.

SCENE ELEVEN

The brothel. EDIE *is knitting in the window.* GUNTHER *is stretching his back as the sun beats down.*

EDIE: Did the Sobbing Woman stop you sleeping?
GUNTHER: It's my back. Lena says I was very restless last night.

> *He gingerly touches his foot.*

And this foot's getting worse.
EDIE: You're in the wars…
GUNTHER: Those dirty dogs really sunk their teeth in.
EDIE: That's some cologne you're wearing.
GUNTHER: I am the owner of a brothel, Edie. I have to smell good.
EDIE: I hope it's cheap.
GUNTHER: Does it smell cheap?
EDIE: If you're going to put the whole bottle on…
GUNTHER: Too much?
EDIE: It's like you're trying to hide something, Gunther. Maybe your wife likes it.
GUNTHER: She was missing all day yesterday.

> ERROL *appears, sucking on a sweet.*

ERROL: Maybe Lena was visiting The Foreigners, Gunther.
GUNTHER: She wouldn't go there.
ERROL: She might have got lost in the mist.
GUNTHER: She knows not to go there.
ERROL: But if she was lost, Gunther—?
GUNTHER: What do you know about my wife's movements? Give your head a rest, moron. You'll wear yourself out with all that thinking. If she's whoring…
EDIE: Can't have that.
GUNTHER: I'm faithful to her. You used to come here all the time, Errol. What's happened? Even a dullard like you has needs. That's why I run this place. Oldest profession in the world. Guaranteed business. How about Edie? Come on. Take her. She's yours.

> *He stares at* ERROL.

ERROL: What?

GUNTHER: You've got yourself a little foreign woman, haven't you?
ERROL: No, no… No.
GUNTHER: Don't want to go sharing a grimy bed with them. I thought you'd fallen for one. Listen to their dirty dogs…
ERROL: I can't hear them.
GUNTHER: [*shouting at the dogs*] Shut up! [*He points at his sore foot.*] I'll come over one night and kill every one of you mutts for this! Those foreigners live too close… They don't complain because they know it.

Sound of distant distorted dogs barking.

EDIE: Their dogs complain.
ERROL: [*laughing*] Their dogs complain. That's funny.
EDIE: Most of the foreigners were born here, Gunther.
GUNTHER: Just because a dog's born in a stable, doesn't make it a horse.
ERROL: How can a dog be a horse?
EDIE: Gunther's a foreign name, isn't it?
GUNTHER: I should go to Noel's to get this boot fixed.
EDIE: Sounds foreign.

GUNTHER *throws* EDIE'*s knitting needles to the ground.*

GUNTHER: What do you think this place is? A retirement home? No wonder Errol doesn't come here anymore. When my other girls do their shift in the window they put on a bit of a show.
EDIE: None of them knit?
GUNTHER: It's bad for business.

AGNES *empties her bucket into the well.*

[*To* AGNES] And so are you.
AGNES: I can almost see the bottom of the river. Not many more trips now.
GUNTHER: You're bad for business.
AGNES: Did you find your way back from The Foreigners last night, Gunther?
GUNTHER: Clear off.
AGNES: You need a cane for that limp.
GUNTHER: I do not need a cane, mad woman.

AGNES: Why? Because he has one? Afraid you'll look like him?
GUNTHER: I don't want you out the front of my establishment.
AGNES: But this is where I empty the water.
GUNTHER: Drink it. Drink the whole river, I don't care. But don't hang around here. My customers see you and they feel guilty. They see consequences.
AGNES: I'm almost finished.
GUNTHER: Give me your bucket! Stop your lamenting.
AGNES: No, no, I need it! Please! You can't take it!

> GUNTHER *takes the bucket and leaves a frantic* AGNES *behind.*

GUNTHER: [*calling*] Clear off, mad woman.
AGNES: I still have work to do! I need that bucket… What, am I to use my hands? It's my lucky charm. It's my bucket!
EDIE: You should rest, Agnes, you never rest. The river's not going anywhere.
AGNES: The water will win. I don't want the water to win.
ERROL: 'The water will win. The water will win.'

> AGNES *shrieks as* ERROL *laughs.* AGNES *leaves, hysterical.*

EDIE: You're cruel to her.
ERROL: Yeah. Do you want a lolly?
EDIE: They'll rot your teeth.
ERROL: So what, they taste good.
EDIE: You like the sweet things in life, don't you Errol?
ERROL: Yeah.

> *They chew on the sweets.*

Do you love me, Edie?
EDIE: If you like.
ERROL: But you let me pay you. And we never even had sex. Still, you always made me pay.
EDIE: That's my job. I am, I guess, a prostitute.
ERROL: If you don't have to pay for it, what's it mean?
EDIE: You always pay for it, Errol.

SCENE TWELVE

The Foreigners. Sound of the river and dogs nearby. LENA *waits while* ERROL *urinates.*

LENA: Not romantic, Errol, to be pissing. And people live here.
ERROL: Only foreigners.
LENA: Come on, *quigena*. [quickly.]

    ERROL *does up his trousers.*

Don't worry about doing up.
ERROL: Where's Gunther?
LENA: *Heke yago*. [Who cares.]
ERROL: What if he comes past?
LENA: He never come to The Foreigners.
ERROL: Agnes said he was here last night.
LENA: Lie down. I go on top.
ERROL: I don't like it that way.
LENA: I'm not lying down here. I get dirty.
ERROL: So will I.
LENA: People not be, how to say, suspect of you.
ERROL: Is this just a job for you, Lena?
LENA: No more talk.
ERROL: I haven't got my lucky underwear on.
LENA: I have. But not for long.

    She pushes him to ground and pulls down her underwear.

ERROL: I'm not a piece of meat you know.
LENA: [*laughing*] Where you get this from? The whores? Do they say this?

    AGNES *appears, seeing* LENA's *underwear at her knees.*

AGNES: Your husband took my bucket.
LENA: *Yip dettay*, *yip dettay.* [Go away.]
ERROL: Nothing happened. Nothing.
AGNES: How am I supposed to empty the river? Are you going to pull those up?
ERROL: Nothing happened. Are you going to tell Gunther?
AGNES: I know what you do.

ERROL: I was just on my way to work.
AGNES: No, Noel banished you from the church.
ERROL: How do you know?
AGNES: I know everything that goes on in this village. Everything. I'll tell him what you do.
LENA: Nobody hear what you say.
AGNES: He's sick, Lena. He needs to see you.
ERROL: Who?
LENA: I not go back.
AGNES: I'll tell him to come into the village to see you.
LENA: He know not to do that.
ERROL: Are you talking about me?
AGNES: I need my bucket, Lena. I've almost defeated it... the water.
LENA: It not you. It drought.
AGNES: No, it's me. I'm going to beat the river but I need my bucket. You really should pull those up. People will talk. I've heard them. They do like to talk.

She leaves. LENA *pulls up her underwear.*

ERROL: Nothing happened.
LENA: She tell Gunther.
ERROL: She said she wouldn't.
LENA: You don't understand.
ERROL: Should I go now?

LENA *nods.* ERROL *dusts himself.*

We should do it on a bed next time, Lena... Even whores get to use a bed.

SCENE THIRTEEN

The village. NOEL *is riding through the night, clutching his Bible.*

NOEL: 'You must purge the evil from among you. The rest of the people will hear of this and be afraid and never again will such an evil thing be done among you.' Deuteronomy 19, verse 19. I keep expecting to see bodies wrapped in blankets dumped out on the streets, Lord. At least you've not made me sick. No boils or cysts. I trust I have earned the privilege of survival. No immediate hurry, Lord... Must take a day or two to brew up a decent plague. You do hear me, don't you? I'm not just talking to myself? It's quiet tonight. Have you claimed the Sobbing Woman? I can't hear her…

AGNES *appears with her bucket, jubilant.*

AGNES: Another load. Look Noel, Gunther gave me back my bucket.

SCENE FOURTEEN

The brothel. EDIE *leads* ERROL *inside to the back room.*

ERROL: I've been thinking how to get the duck out, Edie. Of the bottle. To solve the puzzle.
EDIE: Errol, if you want to keep doing this you can't complain to Gunther about what happens with me back here. You can't tell.
ERROL: Can it go back to just being a baby duck?
EDIE: This is our little secret… Otherwise I get into trouble.
ERROL: Then it could fit back out the bottle.
EDIE: Is something bothering you?
ERROL: Can you kiss?
EDIE: I don't do that.
ERROL: I just want that.
EDIE: I don't do it. I told you.
ERROL: I'll pay.

He shows his coins. EDIE *takes them.*

EDIE: I'll hold you, that's all.
ERROL: I always repair the boot first then they pay.
EDIE: This is different.

She embraces him. He succumbs then starts to claw at her.

No, Errol—
ERROL: I want sex—
EDIE: No—

She tries to fight him off. He undoes his trousers. They struggle. GUNTHER *appears, holding his Bible. They stop.*

GUNTHER: There's no-one out front.
EDIE: I'm working.

GUNTHER: What are you paying for, Errol? What are you getting?
ERROL: I got money, Gunther.
GUNTHER: [*perusing the Bible*] Have you read this, Errol?
ERROL: I can't read.
GUNTHER: That's a shame. You could learn a lot from this.
EDIE: Can you leave us?
GUNTHER: It's a hot one tonight… Can feel the grime on the back of your neck. Drive you mad, this heat. You like Edie, don't you?

> ERROL *nods.*

Better than Lena?
ERROL: I don't know.
GUNTHER: Too hard for you to decide? [*To* EDIE] Leave us.
EDIE: I think I should stay.
GUNTHER: We're just talking. Go back out front.

> EDIE *leaves.*

ERROL: She's got my money. I didn't get anything.
GUNTHER: You've been getting plenty.

> ERROL *awkwardly tries to do up his trousers.*

ERROL: Have I done something wrong?
GUNTHER: Not easy those buttons, are they?
ERROL: Noel says I'm all thumbs. But I'm not. I've got fingers.
GUNTHER: Does she undo them for you?
ERROL: Edie?
GUNTHER: How many 'shes' are there?
ERROL: Have I done something wrong?
GUNTHER: Does she do things for you? Does she talk dirty to you? Does she make a bit of noise?
ERROL: Is that bad?
GUNTHER: It is when she's my wife.

> ERROL *stops trying to do up his trousers.*

You look surprised, Errol. Are you? Open your mouth.
ERROL: Why?
GUNTHER: Because you're surprised. You're surprised that I know. Open your mouth. Show me your surprise. Go on.

ERROL opens his mouth and GUNTHER *puts his thumb in.*

Suck on it. That's it. I gave you your manhood here at Red Light House. But you're a boy, still a baby boy. It's all beyond you.

ERROL: Have I done something wrong?

GUNTHER: Suck on it. You're out of your depth now. It's all grown too big, hasn't it? For that little mind of yours? It's all trapped in there and you don't know how to get it out. You won't solve it. You can't solve it.

Blackout. Sound of distant distorted dogs barking. ERROL *howls.* GUNTHER *grunts. Lights up.* ERROL *is on all fours, trousers at his knees.* GUNTHER *stands, releasing his hand clutching* ERROL*'s hair, doing up his belt. He wipes his sweat with a cloth.*

Pull your pants up, faggot.

SCENE FIFTEEN

The village. Rain starts to fall. Everyone looks up. LENA *spins with her hands out.* EDIE *smiles.* GUNTHER *frowns.* NOEL *is quizzical.* ERROL *is subdued.* AGNES *drops her bucket.*

EDIE: Finally, some rain.
ERROL: Drought's over.
NOEL: What about the pestilence?
LENA: *Bepetafay.* [Beautiful.]
GUNTHER: Bad for business.
AGNES: No… please, no more water.

END OF ACT ONE

ACT TWO

SCENE ONE

The village. Rain is steadily falling. NOEL *rides his bike through the night, clutching his Bible. There is mist and the sound of distant distorted dogs barking.*

NOEL: Not a soul, not a soul on these streets… Let it rain. Let it pour. Let it purge, Lord… 'When Paul placed his hand on them the Holy Spirit came on them and they spoke in tongues and prophesied.' Acts 19, verse 6.

> *He closes his eyes; trance-like, speaking in tongues.*
> *Aagev nyugef serkeef obtu yerceez vuminat kolpase quiveep…*
> *He pedals faster; his hand down his trousers, masturbating.*
> *Romanei lerte peepete nerschdeef mazee…* Oh yes, yes, yes— [*His eyes snap open.*] No!
> *He clutches the bike handles with both hands.*

No… Keep your eyes firmly fixed on the Lord.

> AGNES *is standing still in the shadows, sobbing quietly.*

AGNES: [*singing to herself*] 'Rain, rain, go away, come again some other day… Rain, rain, go away, come again some other day…'
NOEL: Oh God…

> *Red light up on* EDIE *at the brothel. She is holding a bloodied knitting needle. Her face spattered with blood, she breathes heavily.*
>
> *The Foreigners.* ERROL *staggers under the weight of a dead body wrapped in a blanket and slung over his shoulder. Blackout.*

Forgive me.

SCENE TWO

The brothel. A Bible is on the ground near a dead dog, covered with a blanket. GUNTHER *throws* EDIE *his cloth.*

GUNTHER: Clean yourself up. You're working.
EDIE: I can't, Gunther…
GUNTHER: Errol's taking care of it.
EDIE: What about his…?

>*She points at the dog under the blanket.*

GUNTHER: Errol will dump it after he gets back. Now clean yourself up and get back in the window.

>*He takes the needle and leaves.* LENA *approaches* EDIE.

LENA: You see mad woman? *Sobat* [Sobbing] Woman? She hide from me. She tell Gunther— … What happen, Edie? What happen here?

>*She looks under the blanket and reels.*

EDIE: You know that dog?

>LENA *nods and slowly pets the dead dog.*

LENA: *Gerstut dupde… gerstut dupde…* [good dog] Did dog bite you?
EDIE: It's not my blood.
LENA: Who blood?
EDIE: Foreigner's.

>*She uses the cloth to wipe away the blood.* LENA *grabs her.*

LENA: Who was foreigner?
EDIE: I'd never seen him before.
LENA: What he look like?
EDIE: He was just a harmless old man.
LENA: *Negde.* [No.] He here for business?
EDIE: He'd carried his dead dog all the way here. Someone had fed it meat with broken glass inside. The blood was still dripping from its mouth.
LENA: *Negde.* [No.]
EDIE: I couldn't make out what the foreigner was saying. He was hard to understand, his accent. He lay his dog down right there and seemed to be asking for you. And then…

LENA: *Telta mena.* [Tell me.]
EDIE: Then Gunther came out into the street…

> GUNTHER *emerges from the brothel, unseen by* EDIE *and* LENA.

'Someone kill your dirty dog, did they?' he says. 'Good. Now get it away from my business.' And then the foreigner swung his cane at Gunther. Knocked out a tooth—
GUNTHER: I told you not to go out in this rain.
LENA: *Zavae.* [Sorry.]
GUNTHER: English. [*To* EDIE] What did I tell you?

> *He picks up his Bible on the ground.*

LENA: What you do, Gunther?
GUNTHER: Have you read this? [*Reading*] 'Show no pity. Life for life, eye for eye, tooth for tooth.' Deuteronomy 19, verse 21. Shame the old man had no teeth. Left me no choice.
LENA: Why is blood on window?
GUNTHER: No more foreign clientele. Bad for business. I don't want their kind sniffing around, dumping their trash on my doorstep.

> *He kisses* LENA *and leaves.*

LENA: What he do?
EDIE: He took my knitting needle and he… stabbed it right through the foreigner's eye.

> LENA *slumps to the ground.*

LENA: This village… *eldere bin zig*! [makes me sick!]
EDIE: He went quickly, Lena… I think the shock killed him.
LENA: Why come here? Who want to live here? Why you come to brothel? Why?
EDIE: I came to find the hell of the world.
LENA: You find it. I smell him… Gunther cologne. It everywhere.
EDIE: I wanted to see the darkness so that I could truly know good.
LENA: There no good here. No God. No justice. A wrong is not wrong if right person do it.
GUNTHER: [*calling; off*] Get in that window!

> EDIE *finishes wiping away the blood and looks to* LENA.

EDIE: Is it gone now, Lena? The blood?

LENA: It never go. Where is body? I must see.
EDIE: He had Errol bundle it up and carry it back to The Foreigners.

> *They look to The Foreigners. Sound of distant dogs barking and* AGNES *sobbing.*

They must have found it...
LENA: Gunther find hate like lover find love... As if he make it, as if... he invent it.

> *She drags away the blanket with the dead dog inside it.*

SCENE THREE

The church. GUNTHER *enters, wiping the sweat from his neck.*

GUNTHER: Noel, I'm losing my sole.

> *He tosses his broken boot to* NOEL.

NOEL: It's the sixth day of rain, Gunther.
GUNTHER: That hill is getting steeper.
NOEL: It's happening. He's wiping everything out. Every living creature will drown. Didn't I tell you all I spoke to God? Didn't I tell you He'd listen to me?
GUNTHER: You asked for a plague, Noel.
NOEL: Disease, flood... It's no different. The point is God heard me and, in His wisdom, has chosen a flood. It all makes sense. [*He indicates the Bible.*] 'And after the seven days, the flood waters came on the earth. In the six hundredth year of Noah's life, on the seventeenth day of the second month, on that day all the springs of the great deep burst forth and the floodgates of the heavens were opened.' Genesis 7, verse 10. It's providence. I've been building this boat and He's given me a purpose.
GUNTHER: [*examining his foot*] We were due for some rain. How did Noah live to be six hundred years old?
NOEL: Faith, Gunther. What happened to your foot? Is that a boil?
GUNTHER: Dog bite.
NOEL: Looks infected.
GUNTHER: Probably got foreigner's disease. Rabies or something, for Christ's sake.

NOEL: Blasphemy.
GUNTHER: Sorry, Noel.
NOEL: You should have come earlier. That should be kept dry. Do you have a fever?

> GUNTHER *wipes his sweat away with a cloth.*

GUNTHER: I can hardly sleep with those dogs howling and barking all night… We had a bit of trouble down at Red Light House last night.
NOEL: I don't want to hear. I have nothing to do with what goes on down there.
GUNTHER: I should never have let them into my establishment. They forget their place.

> *He takes a swig from his hip flask.*

Yeah, I'll kill all those dirty dogs out there one night…

> *He offers the flask to* NOEL *who glues the boot.*

NOEL: Bit early for the demon drink…

> GUNTHER *looks at his watch then takes a swig. Blackout. Sound of distorted dogs barking. Lights up on* GUNTHER, *somewhat drunk.* NOEL *checks that the glue has set.*

GUNTHER: Dirty dogs… There's a fever in my foot and a fervour in my head…
NOEL: That glue should be set by now.
GUNTHER: Will this sole stay on?
NOEL: All my boots last for life.

> *He hands the boot to* GUNTHER, *who kisses it.*

GUNTHER: Till death do us part. Never kiss another man's shoes, Noel, they might slip the tongue in. [*He laughs.*] Not this one though. Got rid of it. Till death do us part… I remember saying that once… She was up to no good, Noel. What would your God think of that? Her kind can't be trusted.

> NOEL *looks outside.* GUNTHER *puts the boot on.*

You expecting someone?
NOEL: Just making sure it's still raining.

> *Sound of distant distorted dogs barking.*

GUNTHER [*calling*] Shut up!
NOEL: They are God's creatures.
GUNTHER: They're the foreigner's creatures. You're not trying to tell me God created that lot too, are you? Niggers, Dagos, Boongs, Chinks, Wops, Wogs, Wetbacks, Nips, Spics, Slopes, Coons, Kaffas, Jungle bunnies and Gippos…? Something I said?
NOEL: No, you forgot the Kikes, Gunther. Don't forget the Jews. They killed our Lord.

> GUNTHER *has another drink.*

GUNTHER: That's right. And the rest of them would have too, if they'd been there. Oh, I forgot to mention queers. They're wrong and different in the eyes of God, aren't they?
NOEL: In the book of Genesis, chapter two, God created Adam and Eve, not Adam and Steve.
GUNTHER: Ever thought what it'd be like, Noel? With a man?
NOEL: [*reading*] 'Thou shalt not lie with mankind, as with womankind: it is an abomination.' Leviticus 18, verse 22.
GUNTHER: I like you, Noel. We speak the same language. See the world through the same eyes. Read the same book. And what's the point of a belief if you don't stand up and say 'I believe, whether you like it or not because I know I'm right.' Reckon I'll kill all those dirty dogs one night…

> *He leaves, limping.*

SCENE FOUR

The brothel. EDIE *is carrying a sandbag.* ERROL *picks at his sweets but rejects them.*

ERROL: I've got money.
EDIE: What's wrong with your lollies? I thought you liked the sweet things in life?
ERROL: You're a prostitute.
EDIE: I don't do that.
ERROL: You have to.
EDIE: Errol, I have to stop the water getting in.

> ERROL *grabs her with brute strength.*

ERROL: I'm not a boy! You have to say yes to me!
EDIE: What's wrong with you?
ERROL: I've been punished.

AGNES enters with a bucket of water.

AGNES: Another load. I've come from the river. It won't stop. Must stop soon, mustn't it? I can't keep up. The river's full again.
ERROL: Just give in, mad woman.
AGNES: If it stops raining, I can catch up. I can get back to where I was.
ERROL: You can't catch up. Noel says you've fallen behind.
AGNES: I saw you dump his body out there. I saw you. I know what you've done.

She starts to wipe the blood from the window.

ERROL: You're being punished. We all are. All the sinners. Noel was right. God has punished me. 'It's an unforgivable sin worthy of the wrath of God and an eternity in the pit of hell.'
EDIE: Do you believe in God?
ERROL: I believe in Gunther.

GUNTHER limps in, seeing AGNES near the blood.

GUNTHER: Don't touch that blood, mad woman. It stays on the window to remind every one of them to stay away. Stick to their own.

AGNES backs away from the window.

EDIE: Lena's a foreigner, Gunther.
GUNTHER: How can that be? She lives in the village and only our kind can live in the village.
AGNES: She should be banished back to The Foreigners. She's done a bad thing. You all have.
GUNTHER: You're banished. No amount of rain can wash away what you did.

AGNES leaves. GUNTHER checks his foot, wincing.

Dirty dogs… cat got your tongue, Errol?

ERROL looks away. GUNTHER leaves.

EDIE: What have you done, Errol?
ERROL: It can't be undone.
EDIE: Tell me.

ERROL: It can't be... The move has been made, Edie, can't go back. The pawn has taken the queen. Very rare, don't even think about it. And the king is angry. He's angry and the horse is barking in the stable. Barking like a dog, dirty dog. The bishop's not happy—very mad—in his castle on the hill. Banished, under the nose of God. And the duck's in the bottle and it can't get out.

    EDIE *stares at the distressed* ERROL.

EDIE: Tell me what he did to you.

ERROL: I am a simple man. I am having sex with my neighbour's wife—I am having sex with my neighbour's wife—I am—

EDIE: Slow down, slow down...

ERROL: I can't go any slower! I'm stupid. I have money, Edie. I want to pay you to hold me.

    Silence. EDIE *holds him.*

Noel's right. God got distracted when he made me.

SCENE FIVE

The church. NOEL *is working on his boat.* LENA *appears.*

NOEL: [*singing*] 'Immortal, invisible, God only wise. In light inaccessible hid from our eyes'—

    He sees LENA.

He's not here. He's been banished. Has no place in this church.

LENA: I come to see you.

NOEL: You have a husband.

LENA: I need a good man. *Upe manake religiso.* [A religious man.] *Upe manake ofto Godavay.* [A man of God.]

NOEL: I can't understand all that gibberish.

LENA: I need man of God. One of foreigners, he killed.

NOEL: 'Do not offer as a food offering any animal obtained from a foreigner. Such animals are considered defective and are not acceptable.' Leviticus 22, verse 25.

LENA: His spirit need to be pray for. His soul pray for.

NOEL: You want me to conduct the funeral service for a foreigner?

LENA: *Zige.* [Yes.]

NOEL: Hmm?

LENA: Sorry, yes.

NOEL: [*singing*] 'Most blessed, most glorious, the ancient of days, Almighty, victorious, thy great name we praise.'

LENA: Will you help?

NOEL: They don't write lyrics like that anymore. I'm celebrating, you see. The rain.

LENA: We put sandbags in cracks in village. So dry up here.

NOEL: It's all in The Book. Genesis 6, verse 17. [*He reads.*] 'And the Lord said unto Noah, I am going to send a flood upon the earth to destroy every living being.' Except me. I'm the chosen one. It's going to pour for forty days and forty nights, Mrs Lena. The length of time for all critical periods in redemptive history: Moses, Jesus… Noel. This flood is my salvation.

LENA: That is why the boat?

NOEL: Ark. It's an ark, Mrs Lena. Noel's Ark. To float to safety so I can start the human race again. I'll need to fit animals on board. Two of every kind.

LENA: Do you like animals?

NOEL: Not really.

LENA: Noah was on ark long time until water go down. One hundred fifty day.

Silence.

NOEL: All right, no animals. Maybe I'll take the boots with me… Yes, yes, two of every kind. I'll take my boots. A new people armed with faith, morals and sensible footwear.

LENA: Can we all go?

NOEL: Should have thought of that every Sunday you never came to church.

LENA: Will you bury the man?

NOEL: Why? What's he to you?

LENA: He a man. He killed for no reason. He need peace. It's good thing to do. You give him peace.

NOEL: I'm not leaving my church. I'm never going back down there.

LENA: We need you help in village. Gunther, he anger. He go mad.

NOEL: If you find yourself in a cesspool, climb out and take a shower.

The cleansing has well and truly begun.
LENA: I bring body here? Yes? *Plezay*? [Please.]
NOEL: Leave me alone.
LENA: You are not *upe manake ofto Godavay*. [a man of God.]
NOEL: Don't use that language on me.
LENA: You are not a man of God! I hope your boat sink!

She leaves.

NOEL: [*calling*] Ark, it's an ark! Noel's ark. Get off my mountain. Down, down you go to your lecherous rendezvous. Pray for absolution. Your punishment will come, fornicator. I've told God about you and he's very mad.

SCENE SIX

The village. GUNTHER *clutches his Bible and preaches to the streets.*

GUNTHER: The time for hurting has come. We have to take back our village or they will take it from us. The end is at hand. The battle is fought here. I want to see the menace gone. The Bible tells us there will be a time come when the people from every land will return to their own lands. Hasten that day, Lord, hasten that day.

ERROL *appears, sucking on a sweet. He listens.*

We are the chosen people of God, the kindred people of this earth, mentioned in the Bible. Only people who can blush, show blood in their face, are the true white race of the world. [*He slaps his face hard.*] Blood in the face... if you don't have a conscience, you're not going to blush. The foreigners are thieves, drunkards, miscreants. They live less than human.
ERROL: 'Dirty dogs.'
GUNTHER: Are they a race? Are they a religion? Or are they an attitude? I, for one, don't like the foreign attitude.
ERROL: 'Dirty dogs.'
GUNTHER: Noah was a man, according to the Bible, perfect in the eyes of the Lord...
ERROL: 'Keep your eyes firmly fixed on the Lord.'
GUNTHER: He lived, unpolluted, at a time of crisis. Race mixing, Godlessness...

ERROL: 'Keep your eyes firmly fixed on the Lord.'
GUNTHER: Unholy sex…
ERROL: 'Pull your pants up, faggot.'
GUNTHER: Silence!

He is unsettled but tries to return to his sermon.

That time is come once once more. Every sign is apparent. The rain is falling. The waters are rising. A necessary war is upon us…
ERROL: 'Pull your pants up, faggot.'

GUNTHER is silenced. He stares at ERROL then departs. EDIE watches GUNTHER pass before leaving the brothel, dressed in a long, hooded coat and flat shoes.

[*Calling*] Edie? Where are you going? Don't leave me…

SCENE SEVEN

The Foreigners. Sound of nearby river and dogs barking. AGNES *is holding a candle.* LENA *has a handful of soil and is holding a cane.*

AGNES: Is anyone going to say anything?
LENA: *Negde.* [No.]
AGNES: A kind word? A prayer?
LENA: *Negde.* [No.]
AGNES: Nobody came.
LENA: They afraid.

Silence.

AGNES: The rain's going to douse my candle.
LENA: Go then.
AGNES: I want to stay.
LENA: I don't want to fill hole.

She slowly releases the soil.

AGNES: You haven't told anyone, have you? That it's him?
LENA: Why? What good? Who cry for father of foreign whore?
AGNES: There should be a ceremony.
LENA: Noel say no. No pray in this Godless place.
AGNES: This loveless place… Who loves you, Lena?
LENA: Gunther.

AGNES: No. He desires you but he hates you.
LENA: My father.
AGNES: Who lives who loves you?
LENA: No-one. I like you, nothing. *Hironopega* [Between], between, belong to nothing.
AGNES: Who loves you?
LENA: I tell you.
AGNES: You're wrong. Who?
LENA: Errol… He love me.
AGNES: Then you have everything. One is all you need. The whole village can hate you to the core if you just have one.
LENA: Did my father love you?
AGNES: He couldn't do that. It wasn't safe for him to do that.
LENA: And he not see you again since?
AGNES: No…

Silence.

LENA: I going to have child.
AGNES: Why would you tell me that?
LENA: Nobody I can tell.
AGNES: Whose child?
LENA: Mine.
AGNES: Whose?
LENA: I hope not Gunther.
AGNES: Errol?
LENA: He just boy. It was not meant to be, how to say, problem.
AGNES: Errol's in trouble with Gunther. I told him about you.
LENA: Why you do that?
AGNES: I know about everyone. Just like you know about me. I see you all, hear you all, late at night. I crouch outside your windows, listening to secrets, whispers, the sounds of love. I know what you've all done.
LENA: Gunther no believe you. He say nothing.
AGNES: He believed me. Look what he's done since. Look what he did to Errol.
LENA: What he do? Errol not say.
AGNES: You haven't seen him since the rains came. I know. I know.

LENA: Why would you hurt us when you know Errol love me?
AGNES: Because it was done to me! It's a hard world. Unjust, unfair, unforgiving. I paid for my scandal, you pay for yours. Help me, Lena. Help me with the water. You and I should be allies. We are the same.
LENA: *Negde.* [No.] You are mad woman.
AGNES: When the flood comes, Lena, your baby will drown.

SCENE EIGHT

The church. NOEL *feverishly loads his boat with boots.* EDIE *startles him with her presence, removing her hood.*

EDIE: Going somewhere, Noel?
NOEL: What are you doing in my church?
EDIE: If the mountain won't come to Mohammad then Mohammad must come to the mountain. Are you going to look me in the eye?
NOEL: Proverbs 23, verse 27: 'Prostitutes and immoral women are a deadly trap.'

He continues to ready his boat. EDIE *is uncomfortably close.*

EDIE: You are a God-fearing fool.
NOEL: Fear of God is the beginning of wisdom.
EDIE: What do you know, Noel?
NOEL: I know this village is full of deception and debauchery…
EDIE: Have you got an erection?
NOEL: You're trying to undermine my position with Him…
EDIE: When are you going to confess to your desires?

 NOEL *suddenly presses her up against a wall, filled with lust. He tears her coat open and claws at her body.*

NOEL: Don't look… Do you have to see right through me?

He covers EDIE*'s eyes with his hand before pulling away.*

See what you made me do.
EDIE: Why can't you look into the eyes of a woman?
NOEL: Have you looked into the eyes of God? You can't. You can't bring yourself to, because you shame Him… I'm sorry about your…

He gently adjusts EDIE*'s coat, noticing her changed attire.*

Your clothes... You're all covered up.
EDIE: I've left Red Light House.
NOEL: God still knows what you've done. He knows.
EDIE: Do you want to know, Noel?
NOEL: I know what goes on back in that secret room.
EDIE: Do you? Do you know that I have a client who makes me pretend to be dead? He strips me. Then covers me in dirt. Then pleasures himself on me. I must have died a hundred times in that back room. I've seen the depths of desire, the black hearts of decent men... I have another client who—
NOEL: I don't want to know! I'd rather not know... I have to go. I have the Lord's work to do.

He resumes preparing his boat.

EDIE: Do you think God wants you to abandon this village, Noel?
NOEL: I'm the chosen one.
EDIE: Won't you be taking anyone on your boat?
NOEL: Ark. It's an ark. And no, there's only one of my kind.
EDIE: Your friend, Errol?
NOEL: I don't have any friends here. Don't want any friends here. I know all about them.
EDIE: Did you know Gunther raped him?

Silence.

NOEL: Sodomy is as much a sin as adultery.
EDIE: Errol's a boy with adult desires. He understands the sex. It's the love that confuses him.
NOEL: 'Thou shalt not covet another man's wife!' It's a commandment! It's in the Good Book.
EDIE: I was taught by your kind, Noel. To separate the world... Physical, spiritual. Lust, love. Whore, virgin. They said you must banish one to belong to the other.
NOEL: Who said?
EDIE: They tried to hide me from the hell of the world.

Silence.

NOEL: You're from the convent...?

EDIE *nods.*

You could sail with me when the floods come.

EDIE: Why?

NOEL: God wants me to start the world again. I'll need… a woman.

> EDIE *laughs.*

I'm deadly serious.

EDIE: That's why I'm laughing. Help me, Noel. They need help down there.

NOEL: We should wipe our hands of them. They're doing the devil's work.

EDIE: But is evil what you do or what you allow?

NOEL: Why seek hell? It finds you.

EDIE: I'm out of my depth… Errol thinks he can solve this, like it's some puzzle, like a game of chess.

NOEL: What do you want from me?

EDIE: Stop the rain, or drown with the rest of us. God doesn't want you to survive any more than anyone else.

NOEL: He's all I have. He saves me from isolation. He's going to start the world again with me.

EDIE: Too late to start again. You want to be the saviour of the human race, Noel? Get down off the cross, we need the wood. And go down to the village and be the good man you say you are.

NOEL: But I'm about to sail away on my ark…

> EDIE *regards the boat and the church. She laughs.*

Don't laugh at me…

EDIE: Just like the duck in the bottle.

NOEL: What?

EDIE: It's grown too big to get out. Like those ships trapped in a bottle.

NOEL: What?

EDIE: You'd have to knock every wall down to get it out.

> NOEL*'s mistake dawns on him.*

NOEL: But I can't destroy my church…

EDIE: Not that there's even time. Look at it. Can't be done.

NOEL: Can't be done?

EDIE: It's unsolvable. Did you purposely build your escape vessel in captivity?

NOEL: What am I going to do?
EDIE: Bring them to your mountain. Bring your congregation to the high ground.
NOEL: Can't I stay here until the water rises?
EDIE: Down, Noel. Down you go.

    NOEL *gets on his bike.*

I'll find Agnes.
NOEL: Do I have to save them?
EDIE: Straight down, Noel...
NOEL: Will you be here when I get back?
EDIE: Until you reach the bottom. That's where Gunther lives.

SCENE NINE

The brothel. GUNTHER *is in the window, holding* EDIE*'s boots. Sound of distant distorted dogs barking.*

GUNTHER: I'll kill them, I swear it. My head is throbbing.

    He looks out towards The Foreigners.

[*Calling*] Will you shut up?!

    LENA *appears with a sandbag.*

Where's my whore? Where is she? Have you seen her?
LENA: *Negde.* [No.]
GUNTHER: English. How am I supposed to run a business?
LENA: It too wet. Nobody here.
GUNTHER: Where have you been?
LENA: Bury my father.
GUNTHER: [*examining his foot*] Why won't this wound heal? It's just a goddam weeping sore.
LENA: Nothing. You kill him and say nothing. No guilty.
GUNTHER: I didn't kill your father. I killed a foreigner. You're not a foreigner.
LENA: I kill you, in dead of night. *Gervay, oay dupde.* [You stupid dog.]
GUNTHER: English!
LENA: Why? Why deny my foreign? *Illeke dom forenzwa.* [I am foreign.] Everyone knows.

GUNTHER: I don't want to know. Stop talking. Get out of my head. You hardly spoke a word when we met. Didn't know the language. Didn't need the language. We had desire… The eyes, the breathing, the secret hands. You seduced me with danger, I remember that. I was addicted… To the thrill, the risk, the… beast and the abandon.

He presses himself upon her. LENA *does not respond.*

LENA: You forget the guilt. The look you give me after. You back away. Shame in you. Shame in your eyes. You beg me not to tell. Not to speak. You afraid to be the Sobbing Woman but you cannot stay away.

GUNTHER: You infected me, like a disease. Like a dog bite, like the fever in this foot.

LENA: When you kill him, my father, did you know you do it?

GUNTHER: I knew who he was.

LENA: The foreigner's blood on the window is my blood.

GUNTHER: Then go back to your grimy ghetto. Back to your kind. Leave this village. You are in exile.

ERROL *arrives, standing defiantly at a distance.*

ERROL: Gunther?

GUNTHER: What do you want?

ERROL: I told Edie.

SCENE TEN

The village. NOEL, *on his bike, trying to pedal through the flooded streets. He looks up to the sky.*

NOEL: Stop the rain, sovereign Lord, stop the rain… 'Yea, though I walk through the valley of the shadow of death, I shall fear no evil for thou art with me.' Thou art with me, Lord? I can't feel you listening… 'They heard them speaking in tongues and praising God.' Acts 10, verse 46. [*He closes his eyes.*] *Aegev nzaf queghf kerseef venopagat turniyozac zergeed—*

LENA *is standing in the rain.*

LENA: You sound like foreigner, Noel.

NOEL: I'm speaking in tongues. It's the language of the Lord.

LENA: Help Errol. Gunther will kill him.
NOEL: Go to my mountain, Mrs Lena. Go to my church.

LENA doesn't move. AGNES *stands with her bucket.*

AGNES: Make your God stop. No more rain. Don't you know how close I was to emptying the river? You all owe me this.
NOEL: There's nothing I can do, Agnes. Go to my church.
AGNES: What church? There's no church. He knows what you are, Noel. That you use Him to justify being alone. To make virtue of weakness. He's seen you, as I have, late at night, riding with only one hand. He knows you. I know you. Make the rain stop or I tell what I've seen.
NOEL: He won't hear me.

He pedals on, alone.

I'm alone.

SCENE ELEVEN

The brothel. GUNTHER *stares at a frightened* ERROL.

GUNTHER: That was supposed to be our little secret.
ERROL: We can solve this, Gunther. I can solve this. Just like the puzzle. Like the duck. I can get out and Lena too. She could be with me. I could care for her.

The sound of distant dogs barking.

GUNTHER: You think I hurt her? I'm in control. When I harm someone—anyone, my wife, anyone—that's when my head is clearest. My heartbeat doesn't change. And everything falls silent... I seem to want her, Errol. I can't control that. After all I've shared with you... My house, my friendship, my wife.
ERROL: I love her.
GUNTHER: You love her? She's a foreigner. I've tried to forget... She's poisoned our blood. Taken what was pure and... [*He sniffs.*] Can you smell that? The scent of her? The stench of her? You can smother yourself in cologne but it never goes away.
ERROL: I want you to let me marry her, Gunther, or—
GUNTHER: Or you'll tell everyone I'm a faggot, yes I heard you, Errol.

Have you read the Bible?

ERROL: I can't read.

GUNTHER: 'With their tongue they speak deceit.' Psalm 5, verse 9. I will not be deceived by your tongue.

ERROL: You don't love Lena.

GUNTHER: But look what you've gone and done. Made a fool of me. Every single time you… had her, you laughed at me—

ERROL: No, I didn't laugh—

GUNTHER: Can I finish? You should learn to hold your tongue.

ERROL: Lena is not worth it. You said. She's bad. She's… She's a foreigner.

GUNTHER: What disrespect for my wife. This is 'love'? If it is just a word for you, idiot, better then not to speak at all.

ERROL: Please, let's forget this. I'm sorry. We can forget it all.

GUNTHER: Forget that you think I'm a… queer? Is that what I look like to you? A weak man? Are you here now, overpowered and transfixed by your fear of a queer man?

ERROL: I was wrong. I did something wrong.

GUNTHER: I raped a man. So what? I could have beaten you. But I wanted to humiliate you. And that makes me disgusting…

He removes his shirt.

I don't want your blood ruining my shirt. Hatred is power, Errol. It takes fear and transforms it. Look at you, shaking before me. No hatred to cling to. Just weakness. Renouncing all the things you believe in because of fear.

He gently caresses ERROL*'s face.*

'Wish upon my lips. Lust into my eyes. In my sweet heart, dark desire lies.'

He kisses ERROL *softly on the lips.* ERROL *responds uncertainly until they kiss passionately.* GUNTHER *grunts.* ERROL *starts to flail, squealing. The sound of distant dogs barking.* GUNTHER *steps back from* ERROL, *panting.* ERROL *writhes on the ground in agony.* GUNTHER*'s mouth is covered in blood.*

You want to tell people about me?! You want to tell?! I'll do your talking now!

He suddenly feels sick. The sound of distorted dogs barking.

Shut up! I'll kill all you dirty dogs one day!

SCENE TWELVE

The Foreigners. AGNES *is cradling a bundle of rags in her arms.* EDIE *approaches, carrying her bucket.*

EDIE: [*calling*] Agnes, I found it floating in the water!
AGNES: I don't need it.
EDIE: What have you got there?
AGNES: What are you doing in The Foreigners?
EDIE: I want you to come with me to the top of the hill.
AGNES: You looked like you were gliding across the water just now... Dress billowed up like a sail. You looked like something risen...
EDIE: Agnes, why do you empty the river?
AGNES: I did an evil thing.
EDIE: What evil thing?

    AGNES *looks down at the rag-covered bundle.*

AGNES: I drowned my baby. I've been searching for her since.
EDIE: Why?
AGNES: God's punishment.
EDIE: Why did you drown her?
AGNES: They couldn't let her live in the village.
EDIE: Because she was a foreigner?

    AGNES *nods, humming a lullaby to the bundle.*

So they made you drown her?
AGNES: Nobody made me. I did an evil thing... It was forbidden for my kind to come out here. But I was compelled. I knew he was afraid to look at me and yet I couldn't take my eyes off him. I wanted him to want me.
EDIE: The blood on the wall in the village... Was that your foreigner?
AGNES: I deserved to be punished.
EDIE: You're not a mad woman, Agnes.
AGNES: He never even saw our baby. I did an evil thing.
EDIE: But it was so long ago.

AGNES: Years and years, who knows how many years.

She places the bundle down and unravels it.

Only bones now. And the stone used to weigh the bundle down... I died. My soul died. I couldn't think for the fear. The fear of falling. Falling from favour... The talk. The whispers. The stares... And I thought this stone could sink... the scandal.

She wraps up the bundle and cradles it again.

But the flood has brought you back... This time I drown too.

SCENE THIRTEEN

The brothel. GUNTHER *is retching.* ERROL *has gone.* LENA *appears.*

LENA: I hear scream, Gunther. Where Errol?

GUNTHER *embraces her.*

GUNTHER: I'll protect you from the flood...
LENA: What you do to Errol? Where Errol?
GUNTHER: He swallowed my tongue.
LENA: Who?
NOEL: [*calling; off*] Errol!

NOEL *arrives.* GUNTHER *holds up his Bible.*

GUNTHER: Noel! Come in. Sorry about all the water... My sole's come off again. [*He shows his shoe.*] How about this rain? You're wise to live on a hill. Very wise. Religious man. This is the flood. Just as prophesied.
NOEL: Gunther, what have you done with Errol? Where is he?

The village. ERROL *is staggering slowly, ringing a bell.*

The levee bell.

LENA: Errol...
GUNTHER: Broken...
LENA: The levee broken.
GUNTHER: Don't go.
LENA: I have to clean blood on window.

ERROL *appears, ringing the bell, his mouth covered in blood.*

NOEL: Errol! What happened? Errol? Speak to me.
ERROL: [*struggling to speak to* LENA] Argh ler… argh ler…
NOEL: What's he saying?

> LENA *shakes her head.* ERROL *drops the bell.*

ERROL: [*crying*] Argh lerv… argh love… I… love… you.

> LENA *embraces* ERROL.

NOEL: Forgive me. Come with me. Both of you. I can save you.
LENA: I have to clean window.
NOEL: Follow me to my church. You can't stay here.
LENA: [*to* ERROL] When window is clean, we go to my father grave. And lie. Lie with him.

> *She and* ERROL *leave.* NOEL *and* GUNTHER *watch them go. The rain stops.*

GUNTHER: Noel, listen to that…
NOEL: Stopped… The rain's stopped.
GUNTHER: No more dogs. Must have drowned.
NOEL: He heard me. Perhaps you've all been spared…
GUNTHER: Too late. The flood's coming, Noel… It's so quiet without the barking in my head. [*He calls.*] Why did it take until now for you to be silent?!
NOEL: I've got to get back to my church. Will you join me, Gunther?
GUNTHER: What, walk on water? Stay. Have a drink. It's not over. We have a leather bound book with gold gild edges that says we can't lose, Noel. And we're not going to lose. It's a baptism for us, not a burial.
NOEL: I don't think we're reading the same book.

> *He moves to leave.*

GUNTHER: I have a confession, hear me.

> NOEL *stops.* GUNTHER *kneels.*

I bit off his tongue. I speak with it now. I had sex with a man because I hate men who have sex with men. I hate foreigners and I'm married to one. I hurt my wife to make her love me. And now I'm going to drown like a dog.
NOEL: I have to go if I'm going to beat the flood, Gunther.

GUNTHER: No-one can beat the flood. No-one can deny the flood. And nothing I've done can be undone. Just like the duck in the bottle. It's unsolvable.

SCENE FOURTEEN

The village. Night. NOEL *is riding his bike.*

NOEL: [*to himself*] No-one can beat the flood.

> *The brothel.* GUNTHER *watches the water rising around him. He whistles the tune as before and sucks on a sweet from a brown paper bag.*
>
> NOEL *pedals faster.*

Pedal on. Pedal on. Pedal on…

> *The village.* LENA *is scrubbing the blood from the window.*

No-one can deny the flood.

> *The Foreigners.* AGNES *is holding up her baby's rags and laughing, almost crying.*
>
> NOEL *pedals faster.*

Pedal on. Pedal on. Pedal on…

> *The village.* ERROL *is slowly ringing the bell.*
>
> *Their actions and sounds build to a crescendo as* NOEL *pedals harder. Suddenly, he stops. Silence.*

Will you save us, Lord? Will you save us? Lord?

> *Blackout.*

SCENE FIFTEEN

The church. NOEL *arrives, looking around. It is empty.*

NOEL: Is anybody here? Edie…? Don't leave me here alone.

> *The rain starts to fall again.*

No, no more rain! Stop the rain!

> EDIE *appears.*

EDIE: I've loaded up all the boots…
NOEL: No-one came. I tried to save them but they wouldn't follow me. I have no congregation.
EDIE: Old and new, broken and repaired…
NOEL: But it can't get out. We're stuck here. The ark is trapped.
EDIE: This church can't hold back the flood, Noel. In the end it'll fall and your boat will escape. All your boots will walk away on water.

> NOEL *rests his boot on the shallow water rising in his church.*

NOEL: Nobody walks on water… If I lift my foot, you'd never know a sole had been there… No imprint… No mark… See? The water swallows up where the footprint used to be.
EDIE: But there was a footprint, if only for a moment. A step taken that cannot be taken back. Might as well go on…

> *Silence.*

NOEL: The flood is coming, Edie.
EDIE: Do you want a game of chess?
NOEL: Yes please.

> *The sound of water lapping as they sit at the crate with the chessboard.* NOEL *arranges the pieces.*

The salt is my queen… the spice is my knight, no pawn. No, the vanilla essence is my pawn… The pencil sharpener is my rook or is it the pepper? No, that's my bishop… The glue is my king…
EDIE: How can you know what move to make? You don't know what's being moved.
NOEL: It's complicated.
EDIE: Look at the board, Noel. Barely two pieces the same.
NOEL: But it works. You can still play. Your move.

> EDIE *moves a chess piece.*

EDIE: Checkmate.

> *The sound of lapping water gets louder.* EDIE *looks to* NOEL.

The flood is here…
NOEL: He's forsaken me, hasn't He?
EDIE: His silence is deafening…
NOEL: But if He couldn't prevent all this evil He must be impotent.

How could He just stand by?

EDIE: Suddenly I'm afraid to die… And He brings me no comfort…

NOEL: Where is He? Edie? I have to hold onto something.

They embrace.

EDIE: You've never had a true moment of religion, Noel.

NOEL: I don't know what to do.

EDIE releases him and kneels.

EDIE: Kneel with me. Kneel with me in the water.

NOEL kneels beside her, following her motions of prayer.

Kneel because it humbles you to do so. Clasp your hands together to greet yourself. Close your eyes softly to see. Bow your head to look up in hope. Speak in silence to tell the truth. Pray. Pray for something in you and beyond you, so that they may meet.

They pray then look ahead, trying to hold back their fear.

NOEL: Human existence is pain caused by desire…

EDIE: Which can be overcome by contemplation.

Silence.

NOEL: I've got an erection.

EDIE: The water's rising.

NOEL: Can you swim?

EDIE: Can you?

They contemplate.

NOEL & EDIE: Hmm…

EPILOGUE

The village. Sounds of lapping water. All characters emerge from the shadows.

AGNES: I am Agnes. I am known in the village as the Sobbing Woman.

LENA: I am Lena. I am a foreigner.

GUNTHER: I am Gunther. I am the owner of a brothel.

ERROL: [*speaking clearly*] I am Errol. I am a simple man.

EDIE: I am Edie. I am not, I guess, a prostitute.

NOEL: I am Noel. I am a boot maker.

The lapping water rises to a crescendo as the lights fade.

THE END

www.ingramcontent.com/pod-product-compliance
Lightning Source LLC
Chambersburg PA
CBHW042130160426
43198CB00022B/2963